Father Junipero Serra

The story of Father Serra is a story of love
and devotion and heartbreak that would have
killed men less dedicated to the cause of freedom. Despite the hazards of hostile Indians,
epidemics and near starvation in the wilderness, the little lame friar's dream of bringing
Christianity to thousands of savages in a fierce,
new world came true. Father Serra, who
might have become a cardinal, remained in
the wilderness to be a servant of God. He built
many of the great missions all along the coast
of California, laying the foundations of such
great cities as San Francisco, Los Angeles, San
Diego, Santa Barbara, Monterey.

FATHER
JUNIPERO
SERRA

by

IVY BOLTON

Illustrated by ROBERT BURNS

JULIAN MESSNER
NEW YORK

Published simultaneously in the United States and Canada by
Julian Messner, a division of Simon & Schuster, Inc.,
1 West 39 Street, New York, N.Y. 10018. All rights reserved.

Eighth Printing, 1967

Printed in the United States of America

CONTENTS

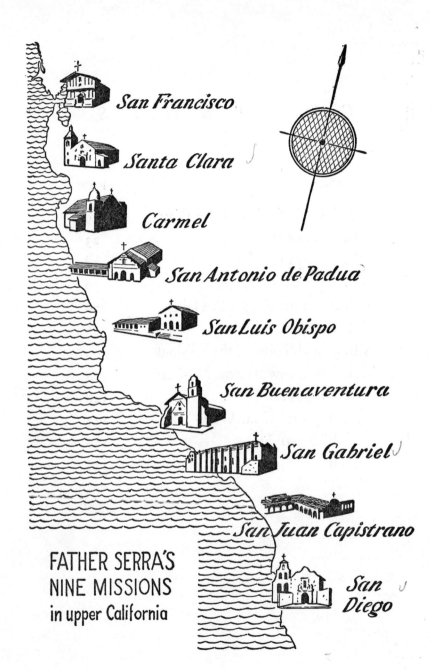

San Francisco

Santa Clara

Carmel

San Antonio de Padua

San Luis Obispo

San Buenaventura

San Gabriel

San Juan Capistrano

San Diego

FATHER SERRA'S
NINE MISSIONS
in upper California

I. *The Beginning of the Way*

"This is sheer folly. You can go no farther, Father Serra. How could you ever have hoped to do missionary work in the wilds of Upper California with a leg like that? Look at it! I shall make a litter and send four men with you to carry you home." Comandante Portolá spoke with his usual decision.

Father Serra stretched out the leg obediently and looked at it with a rueful smile. His face was white with fatigue and pain, but there was laughter still in his dark eyes and the little quirk at the side of his mouth told his exasperated commander that, as usual, Father Serra was finding something amusing in a situation which was not funny at all. He did not realize that his own excitement was the cause of the laughter now.

The leg was a sorry sight, swollen and inflamed from knee to toe, with an open sore from the ankle halfway up the leg.

"It is one of the only two that I possess," Father Serra

answered thoughtfully. "There is no need for all this worry, Comandante. The leg has been in this state, more or less, all the years I have been in the New World. I admit that at present it is a little more. God has called me to preach and found missions and I can trust Him to help me to do the task. He knows all about this handicap and has enabled me to come twelve hundred leagues. Surely, I can trust Him to get me the rest of the way."

"And you will not go home? You should have had a doctor long ago."

"I have had doctors and none of them have been able to help me," Father Serra answered quietly. "This is the first present that the New World gave to me. Father Pedro and I were walking from Vera Cruz to Mexico City when the snake crossed our path. It struck at me and then went about its business in the undergrowth. The walk that afternoon was somewhat of an ordeal and the place has never healed. Wise doctors have told me that most people die of a similar snake bite. God had something for me to do and I lived. The 'something' is here in California and I have not the slightest intention of going home. If I delay you too much, leave me here with a little food and I will follow you with what speed I can."

"And run into Indians and wild beasts, not to mention more snakes," the comandante grumbled.

"I came here to find Indians and I am not afraid of snakes or wild beasts," Father Serra informed him. "Thus far we have seen nothing but desert, and the Indians, who are really important, must be looked for in good earnest. Leave off worrying. I shall be all right."

Portolá pondered. "I am not going to leave you behind," he

said obstinately and turned to summon two of his soldiers, who came running at his call.

"Cut wood and make a litter on which we can carry Father Serra," he commanded them. "Until you can walk again, that is what I intend to do and it is of no use for you to say any more, Father."

"Then I will not." Father Serra leaned back against a rock and surveyed the scene around him.

It was a glorious sight. In the west the sun was setting in a blaze of crimson and gold, the flaming cacti and desert plants greeted his beauty-loving eyes. The camp was being made ready and the men were gathering around the fires drawn by the scent of a cooking meal. Father Serra felt far too sick and weary to eat. He was grave enough now. Something had to be done, that was certain. He could not be a burden on the expedition. Men and animals had quite enough to do without adding the task of carrying a sick man.

One of the animals was in trouble. It was the mule that had gone lame yesterday. The beast was making no secret of its discomfort and was making life as hard as possible for the muleteer by kicks and squeals and struggles—together with futile efforts to bite his doctor. The muleteer was trying to poultice the open sore. Even at this distance, the smell of the ingredients of the steaming mass was overpowering.

Father Serra watched, idly at first, then with real interest. He could sympathize with the mule. If the sore was anything like his own, no wonder the animal wanted to bite and kick.

The muleteer was skillful. His voice was going on in a murmur to reassure his patient. Very gradually the mule grew

quieter. At last a bandage was fixed in place, and water and a nose bag were carried over to comfort the invalid.

The muleteer rose to his feet. "You will be able to go on tomorrow," he assured the mule and then turned to answer the call of Father Serra.

His dark eyes were full of concern as he saw the father's leg.

"My son, you know how to care for your animals," Father Serra said. "What can you do for my leg?"

"I know nothing about medicine, Father. I can cure a wound on a mule's back or a sore on its leg. You need a good doctor."

Father Serra laughed. "The doctors are twelve hundred leagues away and so I must have you. Make a remedy and apply it as you do to an animal. Pretend that I am a mule."

A snort behind him made Father Serra look around. His eyes met the sulky ones of Portolá.

"A good description?" Father Serra questioned, and the grim face of the comandante lightened a little.

"An excellent one," he agreed, and turned away.

The muleteer was still uneasy and unwilling to take the risk, but like everyone else in the expedition, he would do anything for Father Serra. All through the long trek over the scorching desert, when spirits were low, Father Serra could always inspire people with courage and his hand and strength were always at the service of a tired man.

"Go on, Juan," he urged the muleteer. "I need your help."

The muleteer went to work. He melted yellow tallow over the smoky fire and stirred in oil and herbs, a remedy no other man would have dared to try.

Even Father Serra clenched his hands and bit his lip to keep back a groan as the hot mass was laid on his open sore. His face grew whiter still and tears, forced out by sheer pain, made the eyes behind the glasses misty.

He managed a grateful "Thank you," when the leg was bandaged. He found himself lifted in strong arms and laid upon a couch of straw and leaves, which eager hands had made ready. The muleteer's cloak was rolled up for a pillow and a mule's blanket was used for a covering.

Juan brought broth and fed it to Father Serra by spoonfuls and then rose to his feet.

"The pain will be easier soon," he promised. "You will sleep. God grant that you are better in the morning."

"God grant it indeed," Father Serra murmured.

He lay quiet as the waves of pain engulfed him. Pain was no new experience to Father Serra. While he lay he prayed earnestly that God—who had brought him all this way to the land of his heart's desire—would make it possible for him to walk on. A missionary who had to be carried would delay the expedition badly. If the eyes of unseen Indians were watching—and almost certainly they were—would they ever listen to a man who was so helpless?

Oh, these were stupid thoughts, Father Serra decided. There were so many things that he had wanted to do which were out of his reach, things which had seemed utterly impossible at the time. Suddenly, in his own way, God had opened a path here, a friend there, and a great desire had been won. Father Serra let his mind go back to a little farmhouse in the island of Majorca, off the coast of Spain.

He could see it all clearly, the long, low building with the

vineyards and the fields, the flocks of sheep and goats. There his father and mother would be together, doubtless praying for the son they had given to God. How good they were and how much he owed them! "They are saints," he often told himself. "God make me worthy to be their son!"

Here in the desert he thought of the beauty of his boyhood home, swept by the breezes from the sea, steep cliffs rising on the northwest, against which the white foam splashed and glittered in the sunshine. Due north were mountains rich in marble, lead, iron and cinnabar. What fun it had always been to go and watch the men at work in the quarries! Down on the shore were the fishermen who would take a small boy out in their boats with the great sails—sometimes all night, if Mother could be persuaded to let one go. What a thrill it had been to come sailing into the harbor at dawn, the small deck piled high with big fish.

Father Serra was a son of the land. His adventurous life had begun on the stormy day of November 24, 1732. He had been so tiny and frail that his father Antonio Serra had wrapped him up in a blanket and run with him to the village church, fearing lest the baby would die before the waters of baptism could be poured on his head.

"And so, thanks to my good father, my feet were set upon the road to God before I was a day old," Father Serra had told Father Palou, his closest friend, on one of the rare occasions when he spoke of himself.

Miguel José they named him and his father carried him back, holding him close to his heart. The baby's life hung in the balance for many months and the wise women of the vil-

lage shook their heads and murmured to each other that Margaretta would never raise that child.

Margaretta did not give up. She devoted herself to her baby, caring for him night and day, and her unremitting work was rewarded. Strength began to come at last to little Miguel José and he would clutch his father's fingers with his baby hand and pull himself up on uncertain feet.

Of the other members of his family nothing is known. Perhaps he was an only son, more likely he was the youngest child with brothers and sisters who were older and who—by the time he was grown—had married and started their own homes.

He was often ill as a child, and it was only his mother's constant care that saved his life again and again.

These illnesses and the fact that he grew so slowly set him rather apart from the other boys. His life was that of a farm lad when he was well enough, herding the sheep and goats on the mountains, gathering fruit and nuts, taking water and food to the busy harvesters and, whenever he had the chance, staying at his father's side watching what he did. Perhaps it was from Antonio that Miguel José learned to love the beauty about him, noticed the ways of animals and birds and was able to recognize the flowers which grew in such profusion.

The home of the Serras was a happy one. The love of father and mother centered around their little son. The farm was not a large one; the pinch of poverty was felt in bad years— but who minded poverty when they all worked together?

Antonio and his wife were devout and it was from his mother that Miguel José learned faithfulness to his religious duties, to go with her night after night to pray at our Lady's

shrine, to confess his faults regularly, to make his communions and to learn day by day to do everything for the love of God.

Margaretta taught him to be self-reliant. After an illness he must get on his feet. It was from her he learned the secret of the endurance of pain for which he was so noted afterward. Her rule was that he must get about his work as soon as possible. For his mother, Miguel José would attempt anything. Few boys loved their home more than he did.

He was twelve years old when his lack of growth worried him. Much of the heavy work he could not do—and to see the other boys sharing the tasks of the men was bitter indeed. He did not know that people realized that he, Miguel José, was quick and observant and that he was a judge of cattle, sheep and goats. Others might give up when a lamb strayed off· Antonio Serra's lad hunted until it was found. The neighbors discovered that the boy loved each one of his charges and that he would come home carrying the weakest and smallest animal if it tired by the way.

But Miguel José wanted to till the soil and plant and harrow with the rest. It was hard to be told, "You are too small for this."

Miguel José at twelve was just a boy. Like all the rest, he got into trouble. His hot temper would blaze out when he was teased. He would fight his tormentors vigorously, in spite of the fact that he contended against odds. Either he got the worst of the fray or else he was hauled out of it ignominiously by some older lad with "Stop it, youngster. We don't fight people smaller than ourselves."

He could have been unhappy, if he had had time. Fortunately, there was little leisure in the Serra home. Chores had to

be finished early—and from the time he was seven years old Miguel José had had to race off long before the sun was high in the heavens to the school kept by the Franciscan Fathers in the little town of Petra near by.

Here Miguel José could hold his own. "Our little St. Augustine," his teachers called him as they saw his face light up and his eyes shine as knowledge came to him.

Where had this boy gotten his quick mind, his eagerness for learning? the friars wondered. The school consisted of the sons of farmers and fishermen. Most of the lads struggled laboriously with reading, writing and the simple arithmetic needed in their trades. When they had achieved this amount of knowledge, they were content. Miguel José always wanted to know why. He was interested in everything—nature, animals, birds, fish, the stars, the history of the nations and, above all, the wonders of foreign lands.

The old seamen on the beach found him an eager listener to their tales. And what tales they were! The faraway Indies, unknown China, India, all the places to which the tall ships sailed, these were fairy lands to the small boy.

Other seamen had been to the New World and could tell of its wonders: Peru and its gold; the dark, mysterious jungles of the mighty Amazon and, most of all, of Spain's own Mexico. The Indians and their strange ways lost nothing in the telling of the tales and, unlike the other lads who forgot the stories, Miguel José stored them eagerly in his mind and dreamed dreams of faring forth to these far-off lands when, at last, he would be big and tall and strong.

Mexico fascinated him. There were established the missions, which the friars described so vividly. It was not Mexico that drew them, but the Indians who needed to know of God and of the love of our Lord Jesus Christ.

It was the difficulty of getting to those distant lands, the friars ended sadly. It was a three months' voyage to Mexico if you were lucky—more likely, the journey would take much longer, waiting in the windless spaces, day after day, with flapping sails, while the food grew scarcer and worse, and scurvy took its toll.

"But at last you would get to the Indians and then nothing would matter," Miguel José would say. "You would forget the voyage and the scurvy."

The friars smiled at his eagerness. "But you will have to grow up, Miguel, before you go wayfaring," they told him.

To grow! How slow a process that was! At fourteen, Miguel José still had the stature of a child. He worked and exercised in vain. Scrambling over rocks, climbing trees and running races made his muscles hard but did not add the longed-for inches to his height.

He was a part of the village life now at fourteen. He had found that he could hold the interest of the other lads by telling them the stories he had heard and read. Under the trees in summer, around the fire in winter, an eager audience listened while Miguel José held forth.

Tales of the Indies, tales of Mexico and best of all, tales of the saints—especially the story of St. Francis, who was a hero to these boys who loved their Franciscan teachers. Miguel José was asked for that one again and again.

St. Francis, loving and lovable, kissing the leper from whom he had shrunk back, irritating his fellow prisoners in Perugia by his songs and laughter, because all the hardships were for

Assisi and who could ask more than that? His friends thought that many things were preferable and were annoyed at the young man who was entirely happy when they were so sorry for themselves.

It was a story which appealed to Miguel José and one which would bear fruit in his life later. "It is for God, who can ask more than that?" he was to say in days to come.

He was a leader now, though he was unconscious of it himself. The boys followed him because when anything had to be done Miguel was the first to try and do it. A lost calf, a strayed lamb, a missing horse, everyone went out to search. Often the whole party, with one exception, would come back discouraged and unsuccessful.

"But Miguel José is still looking," they would say.

Miguel José was apt to plunge ahead without thinking and get himself into difficulties, lost in the hills, treed by a wild animal or hurt by a fall. But usually he extricated himself somehow and it was but seldom that he came back without the lost and strayed.

St. Francis was a lover of wild things—the flowers, the animals and the birds, even the fierce Wolf of Gubbio. These were his brothers, his sisters, his friends. The boys were inspired to love them, too, but they would just as soon leave out the Wolf of Gubbio.

"Though I don't believe that Miguel José would mind a wolf," one boy would confide to another. "He is not afraid of anything."

Out in the mountains that year, Miguel José was thinking hard. How much he loved learning and yet how little opportunity he had to learn! He had finished the regular schoolwork and had read his way through the small monastery library. When it was possible, one friar or another would give him a little help but they had so little time!

It would be wonderful to be a scholar, Miguel José thought, and yet sometimes his ambitions turned in a new direction. It was a vague desire to belong to the friars, to follow St. Francis and work in his way. It was a very vague idea, for each time it came to him Miguel José dismissed it as an impossibility. His father and mother—how could he leave them? Would the friars ever consider a boy so ignorant and small?

He did not know of the momentous conversation that took place about this time at the school in Petra. It was the Father Guardian as well as the schoolmaster who had sent for Antonio Serra, who had been a pupil there long ago himself.

"We want to talk to you about Miguel José," the Father Guardian began.

Antonio Serra twisted nervous hands. "He is not giving trouble, I hope," he said anxiously. "He is a good boy at home, my Miguel José."

"He is giving trouble in only one way," smiled the schoolmaster. "He learns too fast and he is beyond the school here. We have neither the books nor the teachers he should have, Antonio."

The farmer looked perplexed. A boy who learned too fast— who knew all that the school could give him—was something out of his experience.

"He is young for the farm," he said diffidently. "There are those who say that Miguel will never make a working farmer, but he *does* know more than they think. He sees the points of the cattle . . . he is a good shepherd . . . he notices what should be planted and how we should rest the land. I don't quite know how he has learned it—by watching, I suppose. He does know more than people think," he repeated.

"He would," the Father Guardian answered. "Antonio, God has given your lad a mind and an intellect which should not be wasted; he could go far. Is there any way in which he could go to the University at Las Palmas—can you spare him—can you clothe him? Shelter and food he can have with our brothers there—and a boy like Miguel José will be welcomed by the professors and doctors of the university."

Antonio Serra was silent for a few moments. To give up Miguel José was a blow indeed, yet how could he refuse such a chance for his boy?

"You think he may be a priest later?" he asked diffidently, almost afraid to ask for such an honor for a farming lad.

"The desire for that may come to him, if God wills," was the answer. "What we want for him now is the chance to learn. God gives such gifts as his to but few. What do you say?"

"I will not deny that we shall miss him sorely," Antonio answered. "But it is not for me or his mother to stand in his way. He should go at once?"

"By next week if we can make the arrangements for him. You had better take him to Las Palmas yourself," the Father Guardian suggested. "Then you can see his surroundings and talk with those who will have him in their care. We will make no plans for the future. The way for your son will be clear in God's good time."

That evening was a red-letter one in Miguel José's life. His eyes glowed with excitement as his father told him of this opportunity which had been offered to him and of his own willingness that his son should embrace it. But Miguel José's face fell as he thought of leaving those who were so near and dear.

His father's arm went round his shoulders and his mother's kiss brought him comfort.

"This is God's will for you, my Miguel," she whispered. "Go. Our blessing is with you always."

II. *Las Palmas*

THE days passed swiftly. There was adverse comment, of
course. Why should a son of Antonio Serra be putting on
airs? College, forsooth! College was for the rich, not for poor
farming folk. Farmers' sons should bide by the land, though
a few might follow the sea.

There were others who were pleased and proud; some
unselfishly glad for the boy, others who thought of the honor
done to the village and who wondered openly if he might not
come back someday as the village priest.

The good Franciscan friars were all rejoicing. Miguel José
would do well. He would go far in his studies. They were all
certain of that.

It was a boy half glad, half sad, who fared forth one morning with his father, watching his mother smiling and waving
on the little wharf. She had not let him cry and she was not

23

crying yet. Miguel José was sure she would later on. He was afraid that most likely he would be crying, too.

Las Palmas saved him from it for a time. It was so large and full of wonders for a country boy. And the university seemed a towering affair. But the new Franciscan monastery was a place where a lad could feel utterly lost and alone. It was a very homesick Miguel José who watched his father disappear down the long street.

The friars were kindly, but he could read surprise in their faces as they looked at him. The letters from Petra had been so glowing. What could their brothers have been thinking about to send this child to the university?

Miguel José knew what the expression meant. Why could he not grow faster? he thought wearily. All that he had done to make himself strong, how little it showed!

He had a real fight on his hands now, the longing to give it all up and go back to the farm and home. He was needed there and oh, how he longed for the sound of a familiar voice and the touch of kindly hands. He wanted the sheep and the goats and the old horse he had ridden so long. And oh, how he wanted his mother!

Only Serras did not give up. So Miguel José fought the battle out and won in the days that were so tedious before university work began.

It was hard to see the professors glance at him and then at one another and raise their eyebrows. Still, they motioned him to a seat.

"This child will soon find his level," Miguel José heard one say.

Miguel José did—but not in the way the professors

expected. The friars of Petra had not overestimated their pupil. The lad was passed from one study to another and his homesickness disappeared in the busy days at the university. Miguel José loved learning and here was the great opportunity to obtain it.

He would have been amazed if he had known that his professors were prophesying a great career for him, that in their opinion the most promising pupil of Las Palmas was the son of Antonio Serra.

If he had had time he would have been desperately lonely. The boys did not include him in their sports. He was too small, they told him. Others were jealous of his brilliance. For his first year he walked almost alone.

Little by little, he won his way and gathered a few friends about him, lads like himself who loved books and would pore over them for hours.

"Are you going to the lecture tonight?" one of his friends called to him one day. "It is all about Mexico and you are interested in Mexico, Miguel José."

"I shall be there," Miguel José returned. "Thank you for telling me." He ran off to his class.

He did not know that he had reached a turning point in his life. He still had his dreams of going to far-off lands, perhaps in the train of one of the Spanish governors, who were always in need of clerks and scholars, especially for Mexico. There were India and China too; perhaps some traveler would want a young man to keep his records. The great thing to do now was to learn all he could, Miguel José decided. Then he would be ready for whatever offered itself.

This lecture was different. The speaker was a missionary

who had ability in portraying the land and the needs of the New World.

The missionary, thoroughly in earnest, held the university boys spellbound as he pictured the vastness of the country, the deserts aflame with cacti, the smoking snowcapped mountains and Mexico City itself, trying to be like Old Spain. But Mexico was only a part. To the north lay an almost unexplored region called California and dwelling there were Indians by the thousand to be converted. All this was waiting for brave men endowed with patience, determination and a great love of God. These were the qualities that missionaries would need.

Probably he did not notice the eager, undersized boy who listened wholly absorbed in the tale. New thoughts were crowding in on Miguel José. The vague dreams of travel, exploration and adventure were changing into a call from God. And Miguel José was listening. Someday, somehow, he would go and work with the Indians. With all his might he would strive to make himself ready for the moment when it came.

He said little about it, even to the friars who were his friends. He studied harder than ever. Everything he could find out about Mexico and California was stored in his mind. That knowledge was to stand him in good stead at a later day.

He tried to gain the qualities which were needed, schooling himself to overcome fears, holding fast to his resolution and, above all, seeking God.

Always devout, he was learning much now. Night after night he knelt alone in the monastery church asking for the way to open, offering himself to the Lord he loved—for the work of winning souls.

God accepted him but not in the way he had expected. He was seventeen when the new call came, the call that the young St. John had answered on the shores of Galilee, the call that St. Peter had followed as he dropped his nets and forsook all that he had to follow the Lord.

"Follow me." It was the summons to the religious life, to the way of poverty, chastity and obedience—and to Miguel José the call to become a son of St. Francis and—like St. Francis—to surrender all that he had.

It was not an easy call to answer. Miguel José knew that. Dreams and plans would have to be surrendered as well as other things. He had been thinking of the priesthood of late. His idea had been to start for the New World as soon as that great gift was his. But here was no certainty of missions at all, no certainty of time for the books or the learning that he loved. And moreover, there could be no surety that the joy of the priesthood would ever be his. A friar went where he was sent, did what he was asked, was just what the order decided he should be.

God wanted this. Our Lord had called. The battle was a fierce one but short. Miguel José would obey and follow the path wherever it led.

Again, he did not speak of his hopes and desires. When and how could he follow his call? A question or two told him that seventeen was not considered too young, and while he was wondering how to broach the subject, a way seemed to open. The Minister General of the whole order was coming to make a visitation in the Las Palmas Monastery. He would see everyone, including the boys of the school and those who, like Miguel José, were boarding there while they pursued their studies at the university. This would be the best opportunity of all. No one waited more eagerly than Miguel José for the distinguished visitor.

He watched the great Franciscan shyly as he passed to and fro, greeting the numerous visitors or holding conferences with the friars. It was not until the end of the visit that Miguel José was summoned to talk with him.

His heart beat fast and his hand trembled a little as he knocked at the door and came into the room where the Minister General sat waiting.

Miguel José was at home on the floor of his classrooms. He could talk eloquently and clearly, especially when the subject interested him, but here and now all his self-confidence deserted him. His heart beat so fast that he wondered if he would be able to get a word out. His eyes were eager and pleading as he came forward.

"Reverend Father, I want to be a friar; I want to follow in the way of God. May I come?" he stammered in his embarrassment.

The Minister General looked at him. "You are still a child, my son," he said. "You will have to grow up."

"I am past seventeen, Reverend Father," Miguel José pleaded. "I was told that seventeen was old enough to begin."

The Minister General frowned. "A lie will not help your case," he returned sternly. "Perhaps you have seen your thirteenth birthday, though I doubt it. To say that you are seventeen is ridiculous. It is easy to see you are just a child. The way to God is not by falsehood. Go and grow up. If you are in the same mind when you come to man's estate, if you have repented of this sin and learned to be truthful at all times, you may come again and we will talk more of the matter."

"I know I am small. I have never grown properly. I grew two inches this year," Miguel José said, trying to choke back the big lump in his throat.

"I do not wish to hear any more. Go and grow up," was the answer.

Miguel José stumbled out. It was a crushing blow. He remembered it long afterward.

Dazed, hurt and disappointed, he wandered up and down the streets for hours until, utterly exhausted, he found his way into church and knelt in a dark corner where no one could see him. There the hot tears came and with them new thoughts.

Had he been mistaken? No. Miguel José was sure of that. He had heard the call too clearly to doubt. And since the Lord had called, He would make the way clear somehow. He knew what it was to be rejected and disappointed. Miguel José must go on with his work and wait. Waiting was the hardest lesson at seventeen.

His closest friend to whom he confided his desire did not understand. "They will be glad enough to have you someday," he said to Miguel José. "You have a great career ahead of you. All the professors say so. There are lots of better things to do than to go off to a Mexican mission. You'd just be forgotten there. Here you walk with the scholars. You have the studies that you love. What does it matter about inches if you have brains?"

Miguel José did not argue. It was no use to say it was not books but people that he wanted, that his whole desire was to give himself to God. He would talk no more, only wait.

The waiting was not to be as long as he feared.

"Who is that Serra lad?" the Minister General was asking. "A boy from Majorca? What is a child like that doing at the university instead of the school?"

"He is far up in the university already," several voices chorused. "Miguel José Serra is considered the best and most promising of all the pupils in the university by his professors."

"The professors do not seem to have taught him the value of truthfulness," was the grim answer. "He came to me with the thought of vocation in his mind—nothing extraordinary or wrong about that, of course—but to tell me he was seventeen in an effort to get his own way does not convince me that his vocation will amount to very much."

"He told you no lie, Reverend Father," one of the older friars said. "Miguel José has never grown properly, though he seems to be adding to his height a little now. I do not wonder that you were surprised. We were ourselves when he arrived here three years ago. But for the glowing letters that our brothers at Petra sent to us, I think we should have sent the boy home. We kept him and found that we had a lad who will someday go far."

"Tell me more of him."

"It is a child's body but a mature mind," the old friar went on. "The professors were doubtful about him at first sight. Today Miguel José is working with men, not lads, and is standing high in his chosen courses of philosophy and religion. A scholar he will always be."

"If he has a vocation, would it not be better for him to go to one of the learned orders?" the Minister General asked.

"How long has he been thinking of this, do any of you know? Did the call come to him in childhood at Petra or here?"

"I think he had the idea rather vaguely as a child, Reverend Father," another friar spoke. "Miguel José talks little about himself. I have watched him lately and wondered if some such desire had not come to him. The lad is singularly unconscious of his own talents. I do know that he wants to serve God in foreign lands. I know, too, that he has taken for his ideal our own founder, St. Francis."

"Has he no faults?"

The friars all laughed. The Father Guardian spoke. "Plenty of them. There is the quick temper which is coming slowly under control. There is the equally quick mind which jumps to a conclusion too fast. Also, there is his talent for getting himself and others into impossible situations for which he must use all his ingenuity to get out. He needs to think before he speaks and, above all, to consider before he acts. His sense of humor—a saving grace in trouble—needs control. Miguel José sees the funny side of everything before anyone else. It causes irritation."

"I will make some inquiries about him at the university and then see the lad again," the Minister General said.

At the university the story was the same. Miguel José Serra was brilliant. Very few of the authorities approved of his desire to join the Franciscans. With his mind and intellect, Miguel José might well become one of the leading scholars of Europe, more than one professor insisted.

It was a very different interview from the first one between the Minister General and Miguel José that evening. It was a nervous lad who had come into the room to be met with an apology for the doubting of his word. Suddenly, Miguel José found himself talking freely about his desire for the priesthood, for the missions in Mexico, perhaps even for work in far-off California. Then came the story of his call to the Franciscan life.

"And if you come to us, lad, do you realize that none of these other things may come true?" asked the Minister General. "Have you faced that? Are you ready to give up everything?"

"I have faced it and I am ready," Miguel José answered quietly.

"Then you may try your vocation, my son. If it is not God's will for you, then we shall find it out," said the Minister General.

A radiant Miguel José knelt in the church that evening and the Minister General smiled as he saw him there.

"But do not spoil the boy," was the last direction that the visitor gave as he bade the friars of Las Palmas farewell. "Miguel José can stand hard training. Promise him nothing and try him out."

It *was* hard training but Miguel José squared his shoulders and went at it resolutely. There was little time for books and study in the noviceship. For the most part, too, he worked alone as in his boyhood, for he was too small and slender for the heavy tasks about the farm and too short for the coveted work about the altar and the church. His usual assignment was scrubbing and cleaning the house or helping in the stable or cow barns with the brother farmer. The great compensation was that Miguel José was a daily server about the altar, waiting on the priest as an acolyte. How he loved to carry the missal from place to place, to swing the censer or ring the Sanctus bell!

And at long last he was really growing and when he was allowed to make his vows—though he would never be tall—he had at least the stature of a man.

He had adopted for himself as an ideal a new model—St. Francis was one, of course, but the other was the simple Brother Juniper whose love for our Lord was so great that he could think of nothing else, who was continually in trouble and yet ever joyous because he never had time to think of himself.

Miguel José talked of him so often that it was Brother Juniper's name that became his own on the day when as a novice he was clothed in the Franciscan habit. He was Brother Junípero now—until he should be old enough for the priesthood.

He still had little leisure and Junípero Serra went at his preparation with all the untiring energy which was one of his chief characteristics all through his life. Long before he was old enough for ordination, to his dismay he was elected to the chair of Duns Scotus at the university, never before held by so young a man.

It was an honor he did not want and one which would stand in the way of his personal desire for many long years.

He was younger than most of his pupils—and it was during this period of his life that a young man named Palou entered his class. The two were drawn together and their friendship lasted to the end of Junípero Serra's life. Young Palou entered the Franciscan Order and like his friend he was sent back to his studies as soon as he had made his vows.

Both men had the same idea. Both longed for work in the New World and for many years both met with disappointment on all sides.

There were opportunities enough. The Mexican missions were undermanned and calls for help came to Las Palmas again and again.

With each call, Father Junípero Serra and Father Francisco Palou volunteered and used all their powers of persuasion at the same time.

But the same obstacles were unsurmountable or so it seemed. Minds like theirs were not to be wasted on Indians, so the superiors argued.

Junípero Serra never suspected that his superiors were indulging in dreams concerning himself. They thought he might be the Minister General someday. Yes, he might even become a second Bonaventura, a doctor of the Church, perhaps even a cardinal in time. They did not tell him this. They worked hard to make him most of all—a saint.

Ten years were spent in eager waiting before things began to happen. The appeal came not from the Franciscan College in Mexico City, but from the King of Spain. Missionaries were wanted, not just for Mexico and Lower California where a few Franciscan missions had been started, but for Upper California as well.

A few early explorers had traversed this stretch of land west of the Rockies. Cabrillo had been sent there by Cortés and had found a place in 1542 which he had named San Diego. In 1602, Vizcaíno had discovered Monterey and had erected a cross there and claimed the land for Spain. Nothing much had been done since.

An expedition was now proposed under a comandante called Portolá, an experienced soldier who would take an armed force with him. But the King of Spain and his advisers realized that this would be only an exploration and that the hope of a real settlement would lie with the missions.

It was not altogether in the cause of religion that the Governor of Mexico had appealed to the king: Danger was threatening California and that danger was Russia.

She had moved into Alaska and her ships had been sighted far to the south. There were rumors that she was seeking to expand her territory. It was necessary for Spain to look after her Californian lands. It would never do to have Russia settling as a close neighbor to Mexico. Russia was unknown, unpredictable and, most certainly, no neighbor to be desired in a half-pioneer land.

And so the call was an urgent one. All the Franciscan monasteries in Spain were asked for volunteers. At Las Palmas Father Serra and Father Palou were the first to volunteer and the first to be refused.

"It seems to me that we might as well give up the idea," Father Palou said sadly. "It looks as if God wants us here. The authorities are not willing to send us. We must be content."

"Perhaps we have not asked the right authority," Father Serra answered thoughtfully. "Our Lord seems to have given us this call. Perhaps He is expecting His help to be asked. Let us pray through all the days that the ships are making ready that he will clear the way for us both."

Father Palou agreed. The friends worked and prayed, but the time for the start of the expedition grew nearer and nearer and the opportunity seemed to be passing them by.

One afternoon a messenger arrived post haste at the Franciscan Monastery, a messenger who had come from Cádiz, where the boats were waiting. The first of the chosen missionaries had arrived, he said. They were landsmen and looked at the mountainous waves and the small ships with terror and dismay in their hearts. If the waters were so great and turbulent in port, what would they be on the wide expanse of the great Atlantic?

The missionaries had refused to embark and—what was worse yet—had run away. These were the leaders of the expedition. What could be done? The king's command was unfulfilled. Could some others by found who could start at once?

It was not the king's command that troubled the friars most. The call had come from the King of Kings and the Order of St. Francis had failed.

"Our Father, St. Francis and Brother Juniper would have been the first on board," one friar said, and they looked knowingly at one another.

"We, too, have a Brother Juniper and a Brother Francis," another ventured.

The faces cleared. "We must send our best," the friars agreed.

The grave Father Guardian called a young novice. "Go to the university and find Father Serra," he commanded. "Tell him to leave whatever he is doing and to come here at once and bring Father Palou with him."

The two friars arrived in haste.

"Urgent news has just reached us," said the Father Guardian. "Our volunteers for the California missions have run away in terror of the sea. Will you go in their places?"

Father Serra's glad eyes met those of Father Palou.

"When do we start?" he asked.

III. *Along the Way*

THE start had to be made at once. Father Serra was able to sing the Mass at Petra on Easter Day and to bid farewell to the mother and father he loved so dearly. It was with their blessing that he started for Mexico. The good-by was a hard one. He would never see them again. "Tell them that I am sorry not to be with them," he wrote later to a friend. "The principal thing must be held first, as they know. Tell them that for nothing else but the love of God would I have left them."

There was need for haste. No one was quite sure just how soon the ships for Mexico would set sail. Father Serra and Father Palou spent a discouraging day trying to find a vessel which would taken them to Málaga, where they might set out for Cádiz.

There was not a single Spanish ship in the harbor of **Las Palmas**. The only boat bound for Málaga was an English freighter.

"You had better not take that ship, Reverend Fathers," the agent warned them. "The captain is a skillful one, but his temper"—he raised his hands—"it is truly uncontrollable. He hates all clergy but especially Spanish friars. You will risk your lives if you go with him. In one of his rages he is likely to do you bodily harm. You had better wait."

"That is just what we cannot do," Father Serra assured the agent. "We have no time to waste in delays. We must take this English freighter, whatever the peril may be. God can and will protect us."

"Better wait than not reach Málaga at all," the agent insisted.

"If God wants us for California we shall reach Málaga in safety," Father Serra declared. "All we have to do is to trust in God and see what He wants. We will embark on this ship."

Fortunately, the captain was not there when they came on board, so the two friars reached their cramped quarters unobserved, welcomed doubtfully by the mate, who ventured to give a timid warning.

Father Serra and his companion stayed in those quarters until the ship was well out at sea. Then they emerged boldly onto the deck.

There was a roar of rage and a red-faced, bearded man with huge muscles and great clenched fists bore down upon them.

"Who let you on board?" he shouted. "I am master of this ship and I will have no friars here. I will toss you over to the sharks. I vow it."

"We have paid our passage to Málaga where we leave you," Father Serra told him calmly. "We shall not interfere with you and there is no sense in your interfering with us."

"I'll kill you both," he howled.

"We are expected at Cádiz," Father Palou's quiet voice informed him. "I think we had better get there unless you want to see your ship delayed and yourself inside a prison."

The man stood gritting his teeth and glaring at them. The two friars never moved, and cowed by their stark courage he turned away muttering threats of vengeance.

It was a perilous voyage. During the two weeks that it lasted he never left the two friars in peace. He raged up and down the deck, a knife in one hand and a Bible in the other, from which he disputed dogmas at the top of his voice.

Father Serra was the chief object of his hate. The quiet answer of the Friar to questions hurled upon him drove the captain into a frenzy which once reached such a pitch that he threw himself on Father Serra and attempted to cut his throat.

"It was a miracle that the half-crazed captain did not succeed in his effort," Father Palou wrote later. "God was our protector, for suddenly the captain wheeled and went and flung himself on his bed to relieve himself of the wrath that was consuming him."

There was little rest or sleep for either of the friars after this last attack. They retreated to their quarters, getting what food the mate or the cook could smuggle down to them.

"The man is mad," Father Serra told his companion. "We must take turns in watching, my friend. We must be prudent and never walk about alone. Oh, yes, the madman may kill us in spite of any care, and in that case we shall get the crown of the martyrs without seeking it in Mexico. The mission— God can take care of the mission. If we are lost He can find others to take our places. Also—great as the danger seems to be—He can bring us in safety to our journey's end."

"Málaga! Málaga! Land ahead!" The shout of the lookout was a welcome sound. The journey's end was in sight.

Through the tiny porthole the two missionaries watched the boat come around and sail into quieter waters. They did not venture on deck till the ship was tied up at her wharf. Then very quietly they slipped ashore, only just in time, for the captain was still watching for an opportunity to do them harm.

There was a welcome for the wayfarers at the Franciscan Monastery and a much-needed five-day rest before they embarked for Cádiz in a tiny coast sailboat or xebec. They reached the great port on the seventh of May.

Here at Cádiz came the first of the many delays that Father Serra was to encounter again and again before he would reach California. It was not until the twenty-eighth of August in the year 1749 that he and Father Palou started to cross the Atlantic, together with nineteen other friars.

At best an ocean voyage in the mid-eighteenth century was a hazard, with the storms to be faced and, worse still, the calms which so often held a sailing vessel motionless for days and weeks at a time. There was no way of preserving food, and water was a problem. The lack of fruit and vegetables caused scurvy, and it was usually a group of sick, emaciated and half-starved men who reached their destination. Sometimes a good proportion of the crew and passengers died at sea.

This journey was no exception. It started well enough, and by the end of October the ship reached Puerto Rico, though for fifteen days the water supply had been low and was strictly rationed.

It was joy indeed to land amid green trees and running streams, to eat fresh fruit and vegetables, to rest in the sunshine and regain strength and courage.

Trouble began almost as soon as they left the island. Two days out from Vera Cruz, a storm swept the ship far off her course, crippling her badly and leaving her with broken masts and torn sails.

Though the captain had replenished his stores, as one day followed another these began to give out. New cases of scurvy appeared and the friars nursed the sick, saying nothing of their own discomfort, indeed talking little, for Father Serra had found that silence helped to curb intolerable thirst and his brothers followed his example.

After days of delay and encounters with more storms, the battered boat limped into the harbor of Vera Cruz. The travelers were in Mexico at last.

The missionaries received a joyous welcome. Offers of hospitality came from all sides. Animals and vehicles were made ready for the land journey to Mexico City—and all but three were too weakened by starvation and fatigue to attempt to reach the city by any other means.

Father Serra, Father Palou and young Brother Pedro were in fair condition but just before the start, Father Palou came down with fever and had to be left behind.

Father Serra and Brother Pedro decided to walk. St. Francis with his love of Brother Mule and Sister Ass would never burden them or humble them with himself. His precept was followed in Europe. St. Francis had never visualized distances so great as those of the New World, nor realized that the time would come when Brother Mule and Sister Ass would have to aid in spreading the gospel tidings and be missionaries like their little brothers, the friars. The Franciscans of Spain had likewise never considered such a difficulty and no directions were given as to mode of travel.

Father Serra's was not a wise decision. He had yet to learn the vastness of his mission. He and Brother Pedro started off gaily enough. It was good to be on land again in a country of fruit and flowers, even though it seemed but sparsely populated. At first all went well; it was not until they had to leave the highroad that difficulties began.

There was the time when they reached the banks of a river after nightfall, a river they had been told to cross to get to the town where they could spend the night. It was a deep river and they were at a loss to know what to do.

Help came. A voice called to them and bade them walk along the bank until they were told to stop. Their unseen guide led them to a ford which they crossed easily. Their rescuer was a Spaniard, well dressed and attentive, but a man of few words. When they were safely on their way, he left them.

Kindness they never lacked. A man brought them pomegranates to quench their thirst and once when they were weary and exhausted with hunger, another brought them each a loaf of bread. How good it was! Farmhouse or town mansion, adobe cottage or wooden Indian hut, all were opened for shelter and for welcome.

"We found friends all along the way," Father Serra said afterward.

They were almost at the end of their long journey when the terrible disaster happened. They had come upon a tropical jungle of dense, lush trees and bushes, and they had to watch out for the wild animals of which they knew nothing. They caught glimpses of beasts here and there, but did not know whether they were dangerous. Perhaps it was this very watchfulness which made them forget the peril nearer at hand. Father Serra was walking close to deep grass when suddenly a snake flashed out and he felt a sharp sting in his leg. He cried out and looked down as the snake glided away. He sank down on a near-by rock and looked at the wound, while pale-faced Brother Pedro stood beside him in dismay.

They used what remedies they knew and then pushed on till they reached a village where other remedies were applied. There was little sleep for Father Serra that night, and in the morning his foot and ankle were swollen and an open sore had started, an open sore which never healed during Father Serra's life.

Most people would have given up and would have ridden or been carried the rest of the way, but not Father Serra. A few days of rest, then he went on his way, laughing at his discomfort yet keeping up somehow with his younger companion.

A tired and weary pair reached Mexico City nearly a week later and found their way to the Apostolic College of San Fernando.

The welcome was a warm one, but to Father Serra's dismay he discovered that his fame had preceded him. The rector sprang up with open arms to receive him and cried out joyously, "Oh, that I had a forest of such junipers as this one!"

The snake wound received more attention here, but Father Serra was not a good patient. He was always finding someone who needed help and would wander off to give the aid, when his lame leg needed rest.

He was worried. Mexico City coveted the scholar and he found himself ministering to the rich instead of the heathen he had come to seek. Quite definitely, he did not like Mexico City.

He disliked a church crowded with rich people, clothed in silks and satins, men who were interested in collecting the pearls and diamonds which they strung about their hats, men who ignored the poor and spent their days in pleasure seeking and in idleness. Worse yet were the fine ladies, loaded with jewels, waving costly fans all through the service, sauntering languidly up the aisle attended by innumerable slaves. When Father Serra discovered that the morning chocolate must be served in the church before the ladies would go home, his indignation knew no bounds.

The viceroy, with his elaborate carriage drawn by six blooded horses decked out with silver trappings and jeweled harness, set an example that others followed. What they expected and wanted in a pastor was learning and brilliance; what they were going to get was something quite different, Father Serra decided.

The mission he preached was a grim one. Morning after morning he stood in his pulpit and preached on the horror of sin. Ruthlessly he bared the selfishness, the extravagance, cruelty and irresponsibility of his congregation, so eager in his zeal that the tears rolled down his face as he urged reform.

"You will empty the church," he was warned.

"Better an empty church than a sinful one," he answered sternly.

He did not empty it. Though the women resented his plain speech—and especially his emphasis on generosity, work and the throwing aside of luxury and laziness—the men realized that here was reality and that the penniless friar had what they all lacked—peace, contentment and unbounded love of God and men.

Father Serra made friends. Tall cavaliers jumped down from their saddles to greet him and ask a blessing as he walked the streets. They filled his hands with gold and silver for his poor. The viceroy sent for him and found in him a clearness of vision and a wisdom that made his advice valuable.

Father Serra's chief trouble was that Mexico City did not want to let him go, and in spite of his pleading, months passed before he was allowed to have his first experience in mission work among the Indians. At last the day came when his superiors assigned him to the Indian mission of the Pamé tribe of the Sierra Gorda.

It was not an enviable task. Few men would have found much over which to rejoice. The Pamés were the most troublesome of the near-by tribes and the climate in Sierra Gorda was the worst in Mexico. Missionaries had lost their health there—some even their lives—and few people believed that real progress had been made.

The difficulties did not daunt Father Serra's enthusiasm. Hard work was what he desired and, in his opinion, to win souls was worth any amount of discomfort and suffering. Just as he was about to start, something else filled his cup of joy to overflowing. Father Palou was to be his companion in the mission.

He threw himself into the task with all his might. He learned the language, though he had no gift or aptitude for acquiring a new tongue; for him it always meant persistence and long hours—often stolen from his rest at night. Here, however, he succeeded so well that he was able to write a catechism for his Indians and translate for them the great prayers of the church. He taught the Indians to sing—if it could be called singing.

Father Palou was discouraging. "It's not music, it's just sounds," he protested.

"But our very best sounds," Father Serra answered placidly as he bent over his work. This was a large parchment ruled off with enormous clefs and staffs, with the notes painted red for the treble and blue for the bass. Father Serra himself was pigmented with red and blue, for his paints were home-made ones.

"What are you doing?" Father Palou demanded.

Father Serra held up the parchment. "The singing will go better if the Indians no longer mix up treble and bass," he said. "They have an eye for color and will follow this easily. The day will come when it will be music, after all. And even now, it is for the glory of God."

Father Palou looked dubious, but he went off smiling. What would Father Serra think of next? he wondered. Then his face sobered. Nothing was too much trouble for Father Junípero. How he loved his Indians! "I must seek more love myself," the younger friar murmured.

No stone was left unturned to win and teach the people.

The church was brilliant with candles and decorated with flowers. There were processions such as the Indians loved and, on great feast days, mystery plays were acted by the Indian children, so that those who were slow at learning by rote could see it with their eyes.

Father Serra bettered conditions. The ground was poor and the animals scarce on the peninsula, so Father Serra's first efforts were to improve the soil and make pastures. The sullen, rather suspicious Pamés saw that the mission harvest was twice their own and accepted Father Serra's invitation to move nearer the little monastery and learn the white men's ways.

Here was the chance for further knowledge. The friars taught the Indians to make bricks and tiles by mixing the adobe with wild oat straw. The younger men and boys were given lessons in carpentry, ironwork, the art of the blacksmith and the tanner.

The missionaries did not need to persuade the women. They were so eager for clothes that they crowded about the looms that the mission provided. They would work all day and half the night, if the cloth they made might be their own.

Men and women alike learned to love the lame Father who spent himself so generously for them, who was always ready to help anyone who was in trouble. He was the special friend of all the children, who climbed all over him when he called them to listen to the story of God's love.

California seemed as far off as ever. There was still talk of the expedition, but the fears had died down and with them the first fervor. No one seemed to have initiative enough to push the matter.

Moreover, San Fernando was very loath to give up Father

Serra. He was the first missionary who had been able to establish the work among the Pamés. Why not leave him there within reach of Mexico City where, truth to tell, they would have been glad to have him permanently?

Father Serra wanted no fame. It was a bitter disappointment to find himself still attached to the cathedral in Mexico City and to be summoned from time to time to preach a mission or a series of important sermons.

It took him several years to get rid of his unwelcome task, but at last he convinced the Father Guardian of San Fernando that the two works were more than one man could do. He was allowed to carry his plea for release to the governor, and that plea was indeed an earnest one.

"If the post of cathedral preacher is an honor, it is high time someone else had it," Father Serra argued. "If it is a cross, then it is surely someone else's turn to carry it."

He gained his release and went back to his Pamés with joy in his heart. Now he would be able to carry out his determination to seek them far and wide. He would not be content with those around the mission; he would go and hunt for the scattered members of the tribe, those in the mountains or by the rivers.

Plenty of people tried to dissuade him, painting the dangers of the way. There were mountains, there were valleys, there were jungles to be traversed—and even if these were passed in safety, perhaps the Indians he found would be unfriendly.

"I am on the Lord's business," Father Serra insisted. "God can take care of me and the business, too."

One person spoke no word of discouragement. Father Palou would follow wherever Father Serra led the way.

Father Palou says that they walked over two thousand miles through the wildest parts of Mexico and that in those long journeys Father Serra found his happiness during the months and years of waiting.

Father Serra abhorred luxury and it was his hardness to himself that won the Indians. To them, the ability to bear pain uncomplainingly was the greatest of virtues, and this man who came to them with a smile on his face, tramping long miles in constant pain, filled them with admiration. While Father Serra did not always convert his Indians, rarely did he fail to gain their friendship and respect.

The worst journey was made with Father Palou—partly by canoe and partly on foot—up the river Miges to visit a small isolated Indian village near its source. Father Palou wrote of that journey in great detail. The two friars found sharks swimming in the deeper part of the river; poisonous serpents of every kind crawled on the banks. The puma and the jaguar prowled in the underbrush. The trail had to be cleared with axes, and while they found some fruit now and then, there were no resting places where other food could be obtained.

The mosquitoes rose in clouds about them. Sleep was almost impossible—and they were two weary and emaciated men when they came back to Sierra Gorda. But they were quite jubilant because they had found the Indians and all was well.

People declared that the saints looked after Father Serra. They told him so and he smiled and said God watched over those who were doing His work.

It was on another journey that the story was told of a small farmhouse of Spanish type that Father Serra and a companion found in the wilderness. In it was an elderly man, a young and lovely woman and a child, totally different from the Indians or anyone they had seen before. They made the missionaries welcome. There was a simple meal, a quiet resting place, a peaceful dreamless sleep and little said. Then they went on their way again.

Who were they? Father Serra and his companion were eager to find out. They described the place with the landmarks and the trees that sheltered the house. Father Serra looked utterly perplexed when everyone shook his head and said there was no such house anywhere. Father Serra insisted upon going back to prove his words, but chiefly because he was anxious to see the child again, to get the blessing of the old man and to look again at the mother's peaceful face.

Several brothers said that they would go, too, and with some mules and muleteers they went back. Yes, there was the place that Father Serra had described, with three great cotton trees at the side. But there was no sign of a house or a family anywhere. Thornbushes were growing everywhere.

"There, we told you so," some of the party cried in triumph and then paused suddenly as they saw the awe on Father Serra's face. He knelt in the sand.

"God be thanked," he cried. "He has vouchsafed to show us the house of Nazareth and granted us a vision of the Holy Family."

These were happy days but nothing was being done about California. The fears had died down and the Governor of Mexico was in no haste. Why hurry? There would always be another day. So for seven long years Father Serra waited and longed for the moment when he might again set forth. He was never one to make himself unhappy and gradually it came to the governor's mind that here was one who understood the Indians, a gift that was rare in Mexico or in any of the Spanish colonies. This was the man who loved them, who could allay their fears and win their confidence and trust.

Junípero Serra had courage. He did not covet bodily ease but what most appealed to his Indians was his love and sympathy. Stern with himself, he was patient with their limitations and never gave up, no matter how disappointing they seemed. They knew that forgiveness would always be theirs as soon as they came to him.

Then suddenly an impetus came to the missions. England was extending her territories and her enterprises. Her ships had been sighted and she was sending expeditions to the Far West. She might even colonize there. Between England and Spain lay generations of conflict. It would not do to let her go ahead.

In 1768 the dark shadow that overclouded England rose again. In Muscovy—unpredictable Russia—the czar was talking of a plan to take the whole of western North America, which he claimed as belonging to Alaska and the northern islands.

It seems to have been a rumor or at least some plan that had to be abandoned because of troubles at home, but it roused the authorities in Mexico.

"It is well known," the governor wrote to Madrid, "that the Russians have familiarized themselves with the Sea of Tartary, and that their ships carry on a trade in furs with a continent or island called Alaska, distant only eight hundred leagues from the coast of California."

The distances were great and the measurements erroneous. The idea of geography was very vague. Few knew anything about the vastness of the Pacific Ocean, which most people thought was a large sea connected with China and ending in Tartary.

Other points were conditions in Lower California. Sometime before, a dispute with the Spanish Jesuits had ended in their withdrawal from the Lower California missions. The Franciscans had taken them over but they were ill manned and ill equipped, for the dilatoriness which had prevented the start of the "Sacred Expedition to Monterey" had been a factor in sending proper supplies to the earlier missions.

For once, the King of Spain acted promptly. Two men were sent out, Francisco de Croix as viceroy and José de Gálvez as special administrator. They showed their greatness by working together for the glory of Spain.

Monterey and San Diego must be found again, De Gálvez decided. He went to Lower California and, together with the viceroy, decided that there should be four expeditions, two by land and two by sea.

They would be financed by the money, mules, horses and provisions taken from the missions of Lower California. The next thing was to find leaders.

Portolá, a seasoned soldier who had been governor of Lower California, was one, and with him went a leader who was to do the great work in the unknown land, Junípero Serra.

"He understands the Indians; he is courageous and resourceful, he faces hardships with a gay heart," José de Gálvez declared. "What is that? He is a great scholar; he is an outstanding missioner for Mexico City, we should not waste him on

California? Nonsense. What California needs is our best. Send for him at once."

Junípero Serra was filled with rapturous joy. God had answered his prayers—and he only laughed when De Gálvez looked doubtfully at his worn face and noted his limp.

"God has called and God will bring me through in safety," he said. "When Comandante Portolá starts, I shall be there."

Dismissing the subject of himself, he entered into the plans, and De Gálvez saw that here was a pioneer after his own heart.

The first expedition to go was the naval one to seek for Monterey.

"With the help of two friars we blessed the standards and the ships," De Gálvez wrote happily. "There were two cannon fired and I made a homily myself."

On a bright May morning the second land company under Portolá started off. And with him was Junípero Serra, to whom had been given the presidency of the new missions.

The land of heart's desire was his at last. God had given him the gift of his highest hopes, and all he could think of was that at last he could answer in full the call that always had seemed to be his.

His face was bright, his eyes shining, he was worn with work and toil and very lame, but his lifework was before him.

He was the heart and soul of the expedition, as well as a healer of the quarrels which broke out so frequently among the weary men.

For his own fatigue, for his own pain, he took no heed until he fell in the midst of the desert and found to his dismay that, for the time being at least, he could walk no farther.

This was the man who was sleeping under a mule's blanket with a muleteer's remedies on his leg. He had fallen into deep and dreamless slumber with the certainty that God would bring him through to San Diego, the meeting place of all the expeditions.

IV. *The California Desert*

THE sky was rosy in the dawn when Father Serra stirred and woke. For a few moments, he lay watching the glory of the sunrise, pink and gold and opalescent blue, while all around the colors were repeated in the flowers of the desert.

How beautiful God's world is, he thought and sat up to sing softly his praises to the Creator of it all.

He was better. The swelling had gone down and the throbbing had stopped. He turned with a smile as Juan, the muleteer, came running up with an anxious face.

"How is your other patient, the mule, my son?" Father Serra asked. "This one is better. I can walk on today, I am sure."

"The mule is better but in a bad temper," Juan returned with a grin as he undid his bandage. "Ah-h, this is good—

better than I thought. I will put on more and the Reverend Father will ride, not walk, today."

"I mean to walk, Juan," Father Serra began, but another voice broke in firmly.

"You will ride or you will go home," said Comandante Portolá. "We will have no more of this nonsense. You will obey. Is not that part of a friar's duty, Father Serra?"

For a few minutes Father Serra stared at him blankly. Then he laughed.

"You are right; it is, Captain," he said. "I will obey and I will ride today."

Things went better. A short ride brought them to the mission of San Francisco Xavier and the friars made them welcome. The missionaries had started off from Mexico City with a loaf of bread, a hunk of cheese and a minimum of clothing, but here their brothers sent them off equipped with everything to save inevitable fatigue, with help for the mission to be founded and clothing as well. At Guadalupe Father Juan Sancho provided Father Serra with an attendant, an Indian boy of fifteen who could speak Spanish and many Indian dialects as well.

"Fray Juan clothed him for me with leather jacket and boots, and gave him besides a saddle mule with which he was well content," Father Serra wrote in his brief diary.

At Velicata they founded a mission, leaving Father Miguel and two soldiers to care for it, hoping that in this way the Indians farther on would lose their fears and the news of the white man's mission would be spread among them.

Thus far, the most discouraging thing was that there was no sign of an Indian anywhere. The soldiers did not regret this, but to Father Serra and his companions it was a real problem. How were you to convert Indians if they did not show themselves or stay to be converted?

One morning just after they had broken camp and had started on the day's march the first Indians made their appearance. There were ten men and two boys, and to Father Serra's astonishment they had no clothes whatsoever.

"They were not conscious of any difference between themselves and us," he wrote that night. "I supplied them with figs and raisins which they ate with eagerness and, in return, they made an offering of fish, very rotten and evil smelling."

They were in pioneer country now, but it was a land of green pastures and running waters, where they slept under the brilliant stars, though they woke sometimes to hear the cry of a mountain lion prowling near the camp.

Father Serra loved it all—and noted in his diary the sight of the little rabbits running about and the herds of deer that fed near the travelers quite unafraid.

There were difficulties, of course. He tells the tale of the bad-tempered Genoese cook who killed a poor she-ass who got in his way. Portolá sentenced the man to pay four times the value of the animal and to walk the rest of the way—and this time Father Serra begged for no mitigation of the penalty, for he loved all animals dearly.

A few Indians were seen and Portolá tried to question them, but the language was a difficulty. Even the boy Joseph knew only a few words. One young Indian hunter fought so fiercely that the soldiers were obliged to bind him to bring him into the camp. Father Serra rescued him.

"Even after I had loosened his bonds and assured him that

no harm would come to him, he was greatly disturbed," the diary records. "He carried a bow and arrows, he was absolutely naked, and his long hair was bound with a bright blue cord of some woolen stuff, very well made. He said his name was Axajui. We gave him dried meat, tortillas and figs which he ate suspiciously and with unmistakable fear."

Meeting the squaws was another event. Father Serra came upon two of them in the woods. "They were talking vivaciously and rapidly, as is the custom of their sex," he noted. "They are so honestly covered that I could but wish that Christian ladies were as modest."

How he loved the Indians! "Their grace, vigor, friendliness and gaiety are charming," he wrote. "They have given us fish and mussels and have danced for our entertainment. Our mules terrify them and nothing will induce them to approach one. We must win them."

That was Father Serra's fervent prayer always and it was answered sooner than he expected. The Indians lost their fears and followed the white men, growing more and more curious as they became more familiar. They were no longer frightened of the mules. They found out that it was easy to terrify the animals.

This last discovery seemed a fascinating game and they proceeded to use their new-found knowledge. They would charge down on the camp or the line of march uttering wild war whoops. Then they would laugh and dance delightedly as the heavily laden beasts scattered in all directions and soldiers and muleteers rushed hither and yon after their charges. It took hours sometimes to herd them in, only to have the whole performance repeated a mile farther on.

The Indians had better find out about something else, Portolá decided. The next time the game was started, all the soldiers fired their muskets in the air. The red men scattered faster than the mules.

"It was a necessary measure," Father Serra wrote rather sadly in his book that night. "Still I cannot help feeling that this demonstration of our power has left the Indians in doubt of our affection."

Father Serra spent much time and thought in studying these Indians. The fierce Aztecs, the sulky Pamés and the other quieter Mexican tribes, every Spaniard knew. But these primitive coast tribes were different, childish and simple, lighthearted and seemingly lightheaded as well.

The worst handicap was that their dialect was entirely different from that of the Pamés which Father Serra knew or the language of the Lower California tribe of which his boy Joseph was a member. Nor were these new Indians quick at understanding signs.

Portolá had been bidden to make peace with them. He did not like them very much and his soldiers watched their antics with disciplined endurance. It was the friars who made friends and who viewed them with sympathy and compassion.

"The Indians have stolen my heart away," Father Serra wrote, though he knew well that they would have stolen everything else if they could.

They were shameless beggars. They tried to get the brown robes of the friars as well as Portolá's leather jerkin and boots. They wandered off with anything left unguarded, passing it skillfully from hand to hand until it disappeared.

The most disastrous loss was Father Serra's own. A group

of Indian men and boys gathered around him to touch his spectacles and see what the strange thing in front of a white man's eyes could be.

Most incautiously, Father Serra took the glasses off to show what they were. Five minutes later, they slipped into a brown hand and then into another and in two minutes Father Serra was standing alone and the spectacles were gone.

To be fifteen hundred leagues away from one's base of supplies, dependent upon spectacles which had gone no one knew where, was a strain on anyone's sense of humor.

There were no talks, no stories, no helping of muleteers that day. With Joseph as companion, Father Serra turned detective. Into the wilds they went, pursuing the Indians, who looked at him impassively and said nothing.

Somehow or other the two made one old chief understand and he pointed vaguely eastward. Up and down through villages which fortunately were close together, Father Serra went—meeting a friend here and there who gave him some sort of direction. The fact that as he went on the Indians seemed to know what he was seeking made him think that his spectacles were not far away.

"But, Father, it is hopeless," Joseph said. "They may be hidden in bushes, in trees or buried somewhere. How can we hope to find them at all?"

At last the unexpected happened. Two squaws were squabbling violently over something. Both were vocal enough, screaming at the top of their voices. The quarrel had gone from words to hair pulling and blows as Father Serra appeared and caught sight of the treasure which was the cause of the trouble.

It was his spectacles. The sunlight flashed on glass and metal as he and Joseph separated the combatants, holding them firmly lest they take to the woods. One explained by signs that the spectacles were a most becoming headdress, the other thought they would look better worn as a pendant.

They were not going to give them up to any passing stranger, but at last, when Father Serra had a free hand to produce two necklaces of beads from his pocket, they consented to an exchange.

Father Serra came back in triumph, determined that those spectacles would never leave his face.

"God only knows what it cost me to recover them," he wrote in his diary. "They were passed from hand to hand and it was only after a thousand difficulties that I got them back from some women who fancied them as a decoration."

Yes, undoubtedly the Indians were a problem and if any possessions were to be safe, watch must be kept day and night.

To add to the troubles of the explorers, they were lost. The maps they had were mostly the work of the imagination. They had not found the Strait of Anian or anything like it. Somewhere ahead was the first expedition and behind or before were the ships at sea.

The morale of the soldiers was at a low ebb. Being lost in an unknown desert was a frightening thing. With the sense of direction gone and the maps useless, how could anyone hope to see home again?

"Be of good cheer, my sons," Father Serra encouraged them. "We will blaze the trail. Let us camp here and rest for the night."

Blaze a trail with no trees? Even Father Crespi could not see just how that was to be done.

"The Indians would not leave the stones we place," he said at last.

Father Serra only laughed. "Get up early and help me place them," he said.

There was no pile of stones the next morning at sunrise when Father Crespi joined his superior. Father Serra had been up for hours and now he picked up two hoes and a little sack.

"Where are the stones?" Father Crespi asked.

"These will be better." Father Serra pulled out a handful of tiny seeds of the wild mustard and scratched a line by the path beaten down by the men and animals last night. "*El Camino Real*—the King's Highway—must be edged with gold. It is the highway of the King of Kings that we are treading. From here it would not take us long to find the trail we left, and in springtime and summer these tiny plants will show us where we trod."

Father Crespi nodded. The soldiers came out and stared, then ran for hoes and helped to scatter the seeds. Even the grave comandante came and nodded approvingly.

"One of your best ideas, Father Serra," he said. "*El Camino Real?* Is that what you are calling it? Well, it is a good name, better than any other, I think. You have brought new hope to the soldiers. Now we will go on."

It was the worst part of the journey which they had yet encountered. Portolá plodded on through sand and underbrush, over rocks and low hills. Always they were seeking water and only when they found it could they encamp. They marked these places with crosses and gave them names.

"On the Feast of St. Anthony of Padua, we rose early and Mass was said before daybreak. At six we started, having sent men ahead to look for running water or for water holes. The road ended after a league or two and our beasts drank all the water out of two holes—leaving us with none for cooking— and we found it almost impossible to push on. In memory of these troubles—or favors—sent from heaven, we wished to call the place San Antonio-of-the-hardships but the most miraculous saint desired to temper our trials with consolations. Word was brought back by our explorers that tomorrow we should reach two good watering places, one of them three leagues and one of them five leagues away. Both have clear running streams with pasture for the beasts. Blessed be God." So reads the diary.

Oh, the joy of that water and pasturage when at last they were reached! From there things were easier for a time, and three days later they reached a spot so beautiful and so fertile that Father Serra declared that it was a place not only for a mission but for a city, a city within sight of the mountains and within sound of the sea. "Let us dedicate it to our miraculous saint," he said. "Thus shall we make amends to him for our lack of confidence."

The greenness of the land which grew fairer every day brought joy to Father Serra's beauty-loving soul. The flowers growing by the waterside were his especial delight, a gift for the lowly from God Himself. There were vines heavy with unripe grapes—and above all roses, the flower to thrill a Spaniard's heart.

"Today we have seen the queen of all flowers, the rose of Castile," Father Serra noted. "I have before me now a branch with three perfect blossoms, others half blown and six yet unpetaled. I would I could distill and preserve their fragrance. God be thanked for the joy that He has given to me in these."

Troubles were still theirs in abundance. The paths grew steeper. They were tired and footsore and as the weariness increased so did the pangs of homesickness. Now indeed it was easy to become discouraged and depressed. There were quarrels among the men, prevented from breaking into serious disputes and bloodshed only by Portolá's strict discipline and the example of the Franciscan Fathers, who never complained and who could heal hurt feelings and appease those who felt themselves insulted. The friars never doubted but that somehow or other they would reach their destination.

The journey was variable. "Half walking, half creeping, stumbling and scrambling to our feet only to fall again, we made our toilsome way into the valley," Father Serra wrote in his diary. That experience was not a single one but was repeated from time to time.

The soldiers were discontented but their commander held them.

Indians whom they had brought from Mexico and Lower California were another matter. Once a fertile land was reached, they slipped away to seek a less arduous life, possibly with the tribes in the neighborhood.

"After noon, all having eaten, nine Indians of those who had accompanied us deserted," Father Serra notes, "six from the mission of San Borja and three from that of Santa Maria de Los Angeles. Inquiring of those that have been left to us what was the cause of this unlooked for news, as they were given food, were treated well and always showed themselves contented, they answer they do not know and that they only suspect that thinking themselves near San Diego, they feared lest they should be made to settle there, without being permitted to return to their missions. God, our Lord, bless them, as well for the good they have served us, as for the lack they will be to us in the future."

The expedition traveled on. The signal that they were on the right track at last was an odd one. Two Indians stood on the hills they were approaching, one of them wearing a blue cotton tunic.

"He is from San Diego," Portolá cried excitedly. "He must come from Captain Rivera. He carried the blue tunics, such as the Indian is wearing, and also bales of the same cloth. Our good Gálvez, when he made his first expedition to Lower California, declared that the Indians must be clad and speedily. Some Frenchmen had just asked permission to come to Lower California to watch the transit of Venus, and Gálvez gave orders that all the Indians should be given blue tunics. He said it would be an unspeakable humiliation for Spain if the Frenchmen should find our king's Indian subjects wandering about unclad. This cloth was bought at the time. All that was left was given to Rivera and we were told to see that the cloth was distributed far and wide."

"It will be, if the Indians get their hands on it," one soldier murmured gloomily. "And they will not use it for tunics," he added.

The two Indians approached. They spoke a little Spanish and made some intelligible signs. The white men were ahead, they told the wayfarers, and so were the ships, two of them.

It was two days' journey on. There were many friars, they indicated. They would lead the way to a stopping place.

They kept their word—and after the weary days in the arid, hot desert the explorers came out on a scene of loveliness. The cool breezes from the sea swept over the place; there was abundance of water and the animals drank from the pools while the weary men sought the cold springs that gushed from the rocks. Great trees formed a natural shelter and strange flowers bloomed around them.

Father Serra reveled in the beauty. "Here someday we will build a mission to San Antonio," he declared. "If San Diego is only two days' journey away, what a glorious neighbor San Antonio will be."

The two Indians left them. As far as anyone could understand, they wished to go and announce the coming of the second expedition to Captain Rivera.

The next day Portolá started on. It was well that the travelers had the hope of the closeness of their journey's end, for this last part of the trail proved to be the worst of all. The way led up and down hill, the long slopes treacherous for the animals. Fortunately, there was drinking water, and a glimpse of the sea between two hills encouraged the soldiers to go on.

Three more Indians ran away, leaving the expedition sorely depleted. But they struggled on, climbing for three long hours. From there things grew worse. Even Father Serra's gay courage changed to grim endurance.

Broken and rock-strewn country, it was so bad that Father Serra wrote to his friends that sometimes he feared his heart would stop beating from sheer terror. There were great precipices around which they had to wind a perilous way, and there were long, smooth slopes to the valleys where every step had to be watched. One misstep would be fatal. And they all had to help the mules and horses, who seemed as terrorized as the men. It seemed hopeless at times, and they wondered how long they could go on that way.

The hero, the one who kept them together, was a sergeant, who went on ahead, exploring the way singlehanded. He ran into a band of armed Indians, but somehow persuaded them that he was a friend and came back safely.

"Come on, my comandante, come on," he cried one morning. He was standing on top of a little hill pointing excitedly westward. Eagerly they made their way to him, followed his pointing finger and broke into loud shouts.

There was the blue Pacific—and there riding at anchor were the two ships, the *San Carlos* and the *San Antonio*.

"San Diego Bay," Portolá cried. "San Diego at last."

They all crowded up and stood saluting the Spanish flag flying from the mast of the *San Antonio*. There were no return signals even when at Portolá's command they fired a salute. The ships seemed strangely quiet.

"Doubtless there are only guards aboard," Portolá suggested. "The rest must have joined the land expedition."

With renewed strength they pushed forward and now they could see the boats more clearly. Again they fired their guns. This time the mountains rang to the echo of a returning salute.

They had arrived. The Sacred Expedition had entered the promised land. This was California, the goal of their dreams.

They were met now and their hearts warmed to the shout of welcome, to the glad, friendly hands that grasped theirs. There was food and refreshment, and it was only as the two comandantes stood talking and the friars had crowded about Father Serra that the newcomers sensed that something was amiss.

Where were the sailors and where were the captains of the ships?

Rivera shook his head sadly. "There is bad news, Portolá," he said. "Like your own, my expedition arrived in good condition. It has been otherwise with the ships. There was scurvy; the captain and all the crew of the *San Carlos* have died. The crew of the *San Antonio* suffers greatly with the same disease. Added to this, they have not been able to find their goal. They have been up and down the coast in vain. Monterey is lost."

V. *The Founding of San Diego*

"MONTEREY cannot be lost," Captain Portolá insisted. You are talking nonsense, Rivera."

"But I tell you it is, Portolá," Rivera insisted. "We did not find it ourselves on the way here; you did not find it either. Nor did the ships, though they kept up the search far too long. The *San Carlos* has lost all of her crew with scurvy. The *San Antonio's* men are all down with the same disease—and the captain says he believes that Monterey is under the sands of the Pacific. This is a strange land; we really know nothing of it. There are earthquakes and who knows what else."

Father Serra's eyes twinkled. He had been watching the shore, where the maligned Pacific was certainly not living up to its name. Huge waves were breaking on the rocks and the spray rose high in the air. Now he spoke.

"Monterey with its big harbor of which we have had such

vivid descriptions is rather a large place to mislay itself," he said. "It seems to me that the Pacific would have to do more strange things than usual to cover it up completely. I have a suspicion that it is we who are lost and not Monterey, my sons."

"But we are not lost, Father Junípero," Don Rivera declared. "We are here and we know this is San Diego."

"We shall have to look again for Monterey," Portolá said. "It is important that it be found."

He was quite right. The loss of Monterey was serious in many ways. No one knew just where the Russians were or what they were doing. That they had made a claim to Alaska was certain, and that their ships had come down as far as California was also true. And the only prior claim to California was Monterey, where the explorer Vizcaíno had erected a cross and buried beneath it the documents declaring the land Spain's by right of discovery. This had been in 1602, more than a hundred years before. Without those documents there was nothing to prove that Spain had any claim to California at all.

"We have got to find Monterey," Father Serra agreed. "The old maps are unreliable. The place may be above us or below us. A land expedition could go down the coast. A sea one could go up and down."

"You are not going, Father Junípero," Comandante Portolá declared. "I am not going to risk you again on a land expedition. Besides, San Diego is here and you might as well stay."

"Did any of us start on this expedition to avoid risks?" Father Serra inquired. "However, I have no intention of leaving San Diego at present. There is a mission to be founded here and there is work to be done before that. We have to nurse the sick." He rose to his feet. "We might as well begin," he said.

Portolá heaved a sigh of relief. He hoped that Father Serra would not start an Indian mission before there were some means of defense, a stockade and a roof over their heads. Perhaps the sick would keep him busy until that had been accomplished.

Father Serra was busy enough and so were the other friars. There were very sick men indeed on their hands with scurvy, the disease of malnutrition, which caused blindness, deafness and most often death. But with the care and good nursing of the friars, things began to look better. Slowly the sick sailors regained their health and strength, and it was decided that they should take the *San Antonio* and return to Lower California or, if necessary, to Mexico to gather supplies for the mission.

Busy as he was with the sick, Father Serra found time to hew out the wood for the cross and altar which he planned to erect as soon as possible.

The Indians were coming to the camp and he was trying to make friends with them. And he found time to write a letter to his beloved former pupil and brother Father Palou, now in charge of the mission work in Mexico and Lower California.

I left Velicata very infirm and lame, but by God's mercy I grow better every day. The wound in my leg is still open but it gives me no more than the customary pain and it did not impede my progress. At times our journey was hard with many hills to be climbed; but there were other days when the forests were like groves, with broad and easy paths between the trees and running water everywhere. None of us suffered from cold or from hunger. We never journeyed more than six miles a day. The country, unlike our old California, is beautiful and fertile. The Indians are very numerous and seemingly very amiable. They behaved as if they had known us all their lives. The men and boys go stark naked; but the women, the girl children and even the girl babies are decently clad. Everything is in readiness for the expedition to Monterey and the founding of the mission here is deferred until after its departure. There is much more you should be told, but I have reports to send to the Visitador and to the college; and Captain Perez says he will wait no longer.

Your affectionate brother and servant,
Junípero Serra

Ten days later, when the sick had recovered, another conference of the leaders was held. That Monterey must be found was the unanimous opinion.

Portolá and his men had better start overland and try to find the lost port as speedily as possible.

The ships were a more difficult problem. Both were in good condition but the *San Carlos* had lost all of her crew and of the *San Antonio* only half of the seamen had survived the pestilence.

However, Rivera suggested that he and his men sail back to Mexico on the *San Antonio*—lending their help to the shorthanded crew, report the losses and bring back much-need supplies. The *San Carlos* could remain at anchor in the bay.

The plans were carried out at once and Father Serra had watched the departure with mingled feelings. With Comandante Portolá went young Father Juan Crespi, who with his hopefulness and enthusiasm was Father Serra's right hand, since Father Palou had been left in Lower California to take over his new responsibilities.

Other friars had been used to help the understaffed Lower Californian missions, so that the founding of San Diego was left to Father Serra, Father Vizcaíno, a kinsman of the great explorer, and some young brothers.

While the few soldiers left as guards were busy building the huts and defenses, Father Serra and his companions started the mission.

They set up the huge cross of wood and built an altar over which they constructed a roof of boughs. Last of all, they hung up the bell and Father Serra rang it, calling at the top of his voice. "Come, oh, come, all ye Gentiles. Come and learn the way to God."

The Indians came, not to learn but to look. They were still afraid of the white man's magic, but at least they felt sure that the cross meant a god.

Generally, they crept in under cover of darkness and placed their arrows before the cross, the points buried to show the action was one of friendliness. On the cross itself each day the Fathers found strings of the rotting fish, a delicacy the Indians ate with a native powder made of herbs, which rendered the unsavory diet palatable if not healthful.

Hiding behind the bushes, the Indians watched the huts go up and were especially interested in the tiny shack where Father Serra spent so many hours—greeting anyone who came, conferring with the soldiers or writing letters or copying his diary to send to Mexico whenever a messenger could be found.

The Indians would have liked to examine the quill pen and the inkhorn, but after the episode of the spectacles Father Serra kept both safely in his own possession at all times.

What impressed the watchers most of all were the hours that Father Serra spent before the altar and the cross, hours that extended far into the night or began with the dawn.

There he was pleading for the souls he longed to win. There he laid all his plans, his difficulties and discouragements.

An altar under boughs did not content him. Already he had marked out the foundations of the mission itself.

"But surely not such a big one is needed, Father Junípero," the sergeant protested more than once.

"The mission will outgrow this plan someday," Father Serra answered calmly. "The Church must be big enough to take in all that we hope to win; there must be a school for Indian boys and working places for the men and women. The monastery must be able to shelter our brothers when they come."

"Surely we do not need these other fields which you want fenced in," another soldier asked.

"We shall need them for the sheep and the cattle when they come," Father Serra declared firmly. "There must be pasturage for horses and mules as well. We shall need to grow crops for our livestock and ourselves, and we must have room enough to build small houses where we can teach our Indians how to live."

The garden was started. Painstakingly, Father Serra and Father Vizcaíno planted the seeds, the bushes and fruit trees they had brought from California. Although the seeds came up, the bushes and trees disappeared almost at once. The

Indians had decided that these were the white man's vegetables and had boiled and eaten as much of them as they could.

Soldiers and muleteers used strong language. Father Serra only laughed.

"The *San Antonio* will bring us more slips," he comforted them. "We will plant them where we can watch them. One thing is quite clear—we must learn the Indian's language."

It was a task far easier said than done. "For my sins, a language has never been easy for me," Father Serra murmured to his companions as he toiled over the odd pronunciation of the few words they had managed to pick up.

There were no books, no grammar that could be checked and no teacher who could understand Spanish.

"Would it not be easier to teach the Indians Spanish?" Father Vizcaíno asked wearily.

"There must be some way of learning the tongue," Father Serra returned. "It would take far too long to teach them Spanish. They have to be converted somehow."

The Indians had lost their fears at last. By day as well as night they haunted the mission. It was not an undisguised blessing. What they wanted were the white men's possessions. They tried in vain to make Father Serra bestow his patched habit upon them and held onto his cloak with stubborn fingers.

From begging they went to stealing. The sheets from under the sick were pulled away by skillful hands in the middle of the night, swift feet bearing them off before the nurses could discover just which direction to take. Once this source of supplies failed, they took to the water. In the dead of night the canoes were paddled to the side of the anchored ship and lithe, lean bodies hauled themselves up hand by hand to climb the masts and cut large pieces out of the sails.

It was necessary to place a guard there night and day, which further depleted the small force left on the land.

Though they were hungry, they would not steal food, nor would they sit down to eat if it was offered to them. Instead, supplies were piled in a heap and a weird dance with very intricate steps was performed around the pile. When the dance ended they would carry off the food and eat it in the woods or in their own villages.

The dance was evidently meant to protect them from the white man's magic which might be in the food.

"It is lucky for us that they don't want the food," the Spanish soldiers commented. "We would have nothing left if they did."

Food was growing less and less and eyes that scanned the horizon day by day grew anxious when no sign of the *San Antonio* could be discovered. She had not so far to go for the supplies which were so sorely needed. What could be keeping her?

The language lessons were making slow progress. At last the suspicion grew into a certainty that the teachers were misleading their pupils on purpose. There was no way to check anything that the Indians told the white men, and at first Father Serra and his companions decided that the dialect was the hardest they had ever tried to acquire.

It was the peals of laughter with which their efforts at talking were greeted that aroused suspicion at last.

"We are going to school with new teachers," Father Serra announced one day, and led the way to a group of small boys who were running, jumping, wrestling and generally having a good time. They ran to Father Serra at once. Already they knew he was their friend—and presently they all sat on the ground and began to teach the friars to talk. The lessons varied in length. The teachers would depart without any warning and might not turn up again for days, but gradually words became phrases and sentences and—better still—the little lads were picking up Spanish. They were quick to imitate those about them and would dance with glee when the sentences they had copied became intelligible.

Little by little, in the jargon they talked together, Father Serra was telling the lads the story of the Lord he so loved and served, while for them and the older people he left no stone unturned to try to convey what it was all about.

There was a crèche at Christmas time and on all the great feast days processions were made with lights and banners.

"If we could have just one baptism," Father Serra said again and again. "If I could only find a baby to baptize!"

His Indian boy Joseph who had come from Lower California knew of this great wish and consulted with another lad who had been quicker in learning Spanish. The two decided to see what could be done and one morning they arrived in triumph with a group of Indian men. One, who seemed to be the chief, was carrying his baby son. The small papoose was very tiny and—like the Indian children—very still. The small, round black eyes stared up into Father Serra's happy face and the wee hand curled itself around his finger.

In the unfinished church the font had been set up, and two soldiers were brought in to stand as godparents to the little one. The Indians gathered about the font and listened with interest and curiosity to the service. The asking of the solemn questions and the grave replies impressed them, and it was not until Father Serra took the baby in his arms and dipped the shell in the water that the unexpected happened. The father dashed forward, snatched the child away and within two minutes the whole Indian congregation was tearing over the hills at full speed. The pursuit was a useless one. The baptismal party had reached the woods and were lost to sight, nor as far as anyone knew did any of them ever come to the mission again.

"And our Father Junípero is crying," Joseph said sorrowfully. "How stupid they are! Why couldn't they have stayed?"

For once, even Father Serra was discouraged. It was no wonder that he wept. Were his dreams only dreams which would never come true? It was a disappointment that he never forgot. His prayers followed the child who so nearly became the first fruit of the mission.

Of course, Father Serra would not give up. His next plan met with opposition and protests of the fierest type.

"I am going to seek the Indians in their villages," he announced. "I will take Father Vizcaíno and Joseph. Nobody else is to come. No, I will not take a guard."

"If you are not killed on sight by some hostile Indian, you will be murdered for your clothes," the sergeant told him bluntly. "You know Comandante Portolá would not let you go, Father Junípero."

"He would try to stop me," Father Serra agreed, and departed on his mission.

He got into trouble, of course. Not one hostile Indian, but a whole band of warriors surrounded him, waving their weapons. They shouted and yelled and held their hatchets above the father's head.

It was Joseph who saved him. By signs and a few of the words he had picked up, he managed to make the assailants understand that soldiers would be coming with fire weapons —lots of soldiers—should the Father be harmed.

Sullenly, the Indians gave way and allowed the three to go on.

The next adventure was even more perilous. It happened some weeks later. As Father Serra and his two companions were making their way over a new path to a village farther on, a whole band of Indians came upon them. Joseph could not make them understand either by signs or speech. Father Vizcaíno stood biting his lips; Joseph was shivering.

"Unfurl the banner," Father Serra bade them.

The two obeyed him, hoping that no one would notice their shaking hands. The banner was a big one and on it was the picture of our Lady holding the Holy Child. The sunlight caught the blue and gold decorations, and the Indians dropped their weapons and came nearer to look.

They had never seen anything like it. They touched it timidly and then stood back to look. Father Serra was kneeling before it, his back to them. Was this the white man's god who protected all the palefaces and made them wise? Was this the reason these three men could face an armed band?

The Indians asked questions among themselves and forgot their evil plans. Again, Father Serra and his companions were allowed to pass.

The plan for visiting the villages had proved a good one—and as the weeks passed into months, the mission grew. The church was finished, the other building begun, the seeds were growing. Provisions were getting scarcer, however, and San Diego seemed very deficient in the animals which could be hunted for food.

"We shall be glad when our comandante returns," the soldiers told Father Serra. "He has been gone so long. Can he still be hunting for Monterey?"

"Perhaps he is finding other places as well," Father Serra suggested.

"What are we going to do with this vast wilderness now that we have claimed it for Spain?" one of the soldiers wanted to know.

"It is going to be a great land, this golden California," Father Serra answered. "There will be homes and ranches before long and cities in years to come. There are harbors that will make ports for us. The city of Our Lady of the Angels will rise in that place where we camped one night. Here there will be another city, I feel sure. We have mission after mission to found, San Carlos, San Antonio, Santa Clara—I know not how many yet."

"Is your Father San Francisco to have nothing?" another soldier asked.

Father Serra laughed gaily. "It is not for me to dictate to our Father San Francisco," he said. "He will find his own mission when he is ready."

"Where are the Indians?" asked the sergeant one morning some weeks later. "None of them have been around the camp for two days. Up to now we have never been without them for more than two hours. I wonder if anything is wrong with them."

Father Serra was worried, too. Even the children had deserted the mission. He had begun to teach them the alababa, the devotion that had been developed by the Franciscans for pagan or ignorant people, consisting of the paternoster, the Ten Commandments, and the Rosary—together with hymns and simple prayers. It took patience and time to teach it, but some of the children had learned a good deal of it. They had been coming regularly to say it in the early morning and had usually been willing to stay and learn more.

"At any rate, we shall be able to rest for a day or two," the soldiers told each other.

"We shall have to go and hunt for them," Father Serra said. "There must be some reason."

That the sudden withdrawal of the Indians meant danger, all of them were to learn by sharp experience.

It was night. All was quiet in the mission of San Diego. But while the Spanish soldiers had relaxed their watch in the daytime, at night the sentinels kept their usual tasks. Still they did not see the dark forms which crept from rock to rock, from tree to tree and from bush to bush and, almost flat, crawling up the hill.

The Indians were moving to the attack. It was not one of hatred for the whites but was born of their desire for their possessions. If they killed the white men as they slept, everything would be theirs, they argued, and so as the clouds scudded across the sky and the moon shone fitfully, they crept closer and closer.

Suddenly an arrow flew past the guard and the man gave

the signal just in time. Everyone sprang to his post—a handful indeed against the horde approaching them.

There were only four soldiers, but their leather jackets were a protection against the arrows. With them were the carpenter and the blacksmith, Joseph, and a few other men.

Father Serra and Father Vizcaíno took shelter in the old church and barred the doors and narrow windows as the air was rent with the sound of war whoops and the Indians came on at full speed.

The Indians had no guns; it was that fact that saved the defenders, but the arrows came in a blinding cloud. Father Vizcaíno lifted a shutter to look out and was pierced in the hand with one of them, a superficial wound it seemed at first, but it crippled him for life.

The guns spoke—and then suddenly Joseph cried out.

"Father, Father, they have killed me—pray!" he gasped, and collapsed in Father Serra's arms.

There was nothing that could be done. He had been struck in the throat and died in a few moments as Father Serra administered the last sacraments.

Kneeling beside the dead lad, the friars prayed and waited. Who would be next? At any moment their frail barriers might give way. From the barracks and the small fort the guns were sounding continuously, when suddenly the war whoops ceased. There were screams of pain and yells of rage, then voices died to a murmur. There was a scurry and then silence.

"The Indians have gone. They gathered up their dead and wounded and fled," the sergeant said, coming into the church. "Are you all right? What! Is Joseph dead? And you, Father Vizcaíno, let me look at that wound. We have not enough men to pursue the treacherous miscreants. They will pay and heavily, once our comandante comes back."

"We shall have to find out what caused this sudden attack," Father Serra said sadly. "They know not what they do, these poor pagans. It is a case for mercy and not vengeance, my sons."

They did not agree, but a council was held at once. The question of retaliation was not discussed; the danger was too acute. There were few wounds—Father Vizcaíno's was the most serious—and the only death was Joseph's. His burial must be under cover of darkness, the council decided. The Indians might be encouraged to attack again if they knew of his death.

With a sad heart, Father Serra said the Requiem for the lad he loved. Joseph was laid in his quiet grave in the darkness while strict watch was kept.

Father Serra persisted in his effort to win the Indians again. His little lads ventured back first, peeping timidly into the mission, running away, then at last coming to crouch at Father Serra's feet.

It was from them that the reason for the attack was gathered. It had come about from greediness. The Indians had decided that all the valued treasures of the white men might be theirs once the owners were slain, and that had been the motive of the whole affair.

The soldiers were distrustful, but Father Serra knew that the lesson had been learned. There was no begging now and—for the time at least—no theft.

Young men came back with ill-tended gunshot wounds and asked for help. They were cared for, and quite fearlessly the

friars went over to the villages to look after the seriously
wounded. How many had died in the battle the Indians
never told.

The hunters and explorers had said many times that once an
Indian was befriended he was a friend forever, and Father
Serra and his companions were finding it true. Through the
danger, the sorrow and disaster, success had come to the mission. Nursing the wounded had won gratitude from the
Indians—and now it was not only boys and a few women who
came asking to know what it all meant. The language lessons
progressed rapidly, for the Indians wanted to understand, and
soon there were baptisms, not only of children but of men and
women as well.

Still, anxiety was increasing. Where were Portolá and his
men? Provisions were getting much too low. Where was the
San Antonio? She should have cast anchor in the bay weeks
ago. If she had foundered at sea the mission of San Diego
would soon be in sore straits. Morning after morning the little
company scanned the horizon for the sight of a sail and then
climbed the highest hill to look for Portolá and his expedition.

VI. *Lost Monterey*

WHERE was Portolá? Many a time he had wished he knew himself, as the days grew into weeks and the weeks into months.

"Monterey is lost, why did I ever try to find it?" he sighed.

The party had started out in high spirits and all had gone very well at first. The country was beautiful; there were possibilities everywhere. Eastward rose the great Rockies and the explorers came out on plains and deserts flaming with flowers and with an abundance of game. They marched through forests full of enormous trees, such as they had never seen before.

One day they came upon the largest deer they had ever seen, a herd of them with broad, heavy horns—animals who could swim the lakes and rivers and who proved to be formidable antagonists. The Indians called them the wapiti. More aggressive and less welcome were the grizzly bears who appeared from the mountains and prowled about the camp at night.

The two youngest soldiers, little more than boys, made the most exciting discovery as they wandered over to the coast to see what was there. They climbed a hill and looked out, too astonished to speak at first for the glory of the sight before them—waters ablaze with the setting sun, vast waters that the naval explorer who followed them was to declare large enough for three navies of Spain to be hidden from each other.

It was the Golden Gate they saw and they went dashing at full speed to the camp with the news.

Everyone ran to see this great wonder. Father Juan Crespi named the bay San Francisco, saying the saint *had* led them to a spot for his mission.

But they had to leave it now. The traveling grew worse and food scarcer as they trudged a few miles every day. They lost much time going eastward in search of food for the animals, the mules that were growing thinner every day like themselves. Then came a case of the dreaded scurvy and panic came into their hearts. Eyes bloodshot and weary could not even recognize landmarks, and at last Comandante Portolá made up his mind to abandon his search.

He did not know that he was within five miles of his objective and that the water over to the west was the harbor of Monterey.

He erected a cross, carved the words that there was writing at the foot and buried his papers there. Then they started back in what they hoped was the direction of San Diego.

The scurvy grew worse; the food gave out—and though they found water they discovered nothing else. They subsisted on mule meat, half cooked and too unpalatable for any but starving men.

It was a sorely discouraged party which came in sight of the mission weeks later, tumbling in exhaustion upon the grass and begging for food.

They were cared for, fed and comforted, though Father Serra spoke his own disapproval. "You went to Rome without seeing the Holy Father, my son," he said dryly. "You must have been close upon Monterey. Vizcaíno's maps are erroneous, we have discovered that. Perhaps we have overshot the mark in our search."

"There was nothing to do but come home," said Portolá grimly.

"We must try again," Father Serra insisted. "We will have a mission there someday."

To Father Serra's relief, Comandante Portolá had no energy or desire to hunt up the Indian plotters who were responsible for the late rebellion; and for a few days everything seemed to be going well.

Then came the thunderbolt which looked like the end of all his dreams.

"We are going home," Portolá told him. "It is folly for us to stay. The food is almost gone. It is impossible to settle this wild country. The *San Antonio* is probably lost at sea. Monterey is not found. We have no proof that we have any business here at all."

Leave San Diego, the church that he had built, the plants that he had sown, the fields half fenced in—and most of all, the pagan Indians unconverted and those who had been baptized who still knew so little! Oh, he could not! No wonder Father Serra's brave heart sank at the thought of leaving the mission. Such a leaving would be a final departure for himself, he knew.

If the Spanish expedition returned as a failure, it might well be another hundred years before a new attempt was made. No one knew better than Father Serra—from sad experience—the difficulties of getting the authorities to move. Was it for his sins this had come about? he thought humbly. Perhaps he had been too arrogant. After all, was an undersized, lame friar fit for so great a work?

It was not *his* work. And to sit down in despair and depression was faithlessness, Father Serra told himself.

He rose to his feet and stretched his arms wide. "You want California, dear Lord," he cried. "And I want it all for you. I appeal to you, O King of Kings."

He knew now what he would do and he lay down to sleep. He woke in the morning, quiet and confident and with new courage. It was God's work. He would look after His own.

After Mass he sought Comandante Portolá. "Let us make a great novena," he suggested. "Nine days of prayer and vigil will bring us to the feast of St. Joseph. Let us wait that long to see if the *San Antonio* will not come."

Portolá refused bluntly at first. Then he eyed Father Serra doubtfully. He saw the friar's lips tighten and the steady resolution dawn in his eyes. "It is folly to stay," the comandante muttered.

"Go then," Father Serra bade him quietly. "I am staying here."

"Stay here! Do not talk nonsense, Father Junípero. You will

come with us. I am commander of this expedition and I refuse to leave you here alone."

"Father Serra will not be alone," Father Crespi spoke resolutely. "I am staying, too. The work is begun. The Christian Indians are our responsibility. We are staying."

Comandante Portolá blustered in vain. Father Serra and Father Crespi were unmoved. Sulkily at last, Portolá consented to wait until the twentieth of March before starting homeward. "If the food is strictly rationed, there should be enough," he said.

"Later we will talk again," he added grimly. He knew in his heart that it would be useless. He had an uneasy feeling that he would leave behind him two lonely friars to carry on a work undefended by Spain.

The enthusiasm of his soldiers was some small comfort. They began to pack their few belongings. Over the campfires they discussed plans as to how the home journey could be made most swiftly. Lower California first, of course, and then on to Mexico City and the viceroy.

Father Serra said nothing. He looked after his converts, nursed the sick, comforted the sorrowful. At dawn and midday and evening he gathered everyone into the church to keep the novena.

"Holy Mary, pray for us! Holy Joseph, pray for us! Help us, O Lord, and bring the *San Antonio* to port." The words rang out over and over again.

Night after night Father Serra sought the hills from midnight until dawn, watching and waiting. When the sunlight flooded the waters with glory he would scan the horizon.

Seven days passed, then the eighth and the ninth greeted an empty sea.

Yet the feast of St. Joseph was celebrated with due solemnity. The Mass and the *Te Deum* were offered in thanksgiving as if every petition had been fulfilled.

"We start for Mexico tomorrow," Portolá said firmly. "And you, Father Junípero and Father Crespi, are coming even if we have to carry you."

Father Serra did not argue. Quietly he turned away up to his hills again. He had a battle to fight, a decision to make. Hour after hour he paced.

Why was God saying no? Was the mission to fail after all? Junípero Serra had been so sure of God's will. What could be wrong? Should he go? Should he stay? He knew what he wanted, but which was right? Could he maintain his faith and courage in the face of this disaster?

It was a sore conflict but he won as the sun was setting toward the west. He would trust still. God would look after the mission and Junípero Serra did not matter at all. He was only God's servant, vowed to do God's will.

He turned to look at all the beauty about him, letting his gaze rest last upon the sea. He stared, shaded his eyes with his hand and looked again. Was that a *sail* on the horizon?

Joy took his breath for the moment. Could it be? Far out was a ship, a Spanish ship, and as she drew nearer he recognized her. It was the *San Antonio* heading for San Diego. Help was here at last.

"A sail, a sail!" he shouted as he came into the camp.

They all crowded onto the hill and watched. It was the *San Antonio* without doubt. She came nearer and nearer, though it was another day before she cast anchor in the bay. The crew landed amid cheers of welcome.

Supplies were piled on the beach, provisions gathered at every port.

"We were making for Monterey," Captain Perez said. "We landed on the coast some days ago and the Indians told us that you were leaving, Comandante Portolá, so I changed my course and came here to find out if the rumor was true."

He looked around at the buildings which were going up, at the Indians helping so willingly and gladly, at the tired faces of the undernourished men.

"You have done a great work," he said. "The food has given out, you say, Portolá? Well we will land sufficient for your need here. We have seeds; we have plants, trees and bushes— and I see the fields are prepared. Yes, we will stay here to help you and then we will go to Monterey."

"Which we cannot find," Portolá told him gloomily.

"If you have been trusting to the map, no wonder," Perez laughed. "Vizcaíno was a great explorer but he did not know how to draw maps. I think the place was overshot and that we were in the wrong parallel. At any rate, my orders are to find it."

The *San Antonio* was well manned. She had brought sailors, soldiers, artisans and supplies of every kind. Great was the rejoicing and spirits soared high.

Once things were prospering, the expeditions by land and sea were organized. Father Serra was to go by ship.

"Your ship will not turn back with Father Junípero on

board," Portolá told Captain Perez. "But he knows nothing of navigation and perhaps you can keep him quiet so that the sore in his leg will have a chance of healing. I will make my way to the highest spot we reached. You will be able to recognize it, too, for the three crosses can be seen at sea."

A courier was starting out for Lower California the next day, Father Serra discovered, as the summons came for him to embark, so sitting on the deck he wrote a short letter to his friend, Father Palou.

Late last night, the captain sent word to embark and I gladly obeyed the summons. Father Parron and Father Gomez remain at San Diego. Father Juan Crespi is with me now. He is destined for San Buenaventura and I for Monterey. I received no letter by the *San Antonio*, for the captain was directed to go to Monterey without stopping at San Diego. The death of His Holiness, Pope Clement the Thirteenth, and the election of one of our religious, Ganganelli, are rumors which have reached us. If there is truth in them please let us know, and also the new Pope's pontifical name, so that he may be prayed for properly in the Mass. Tell us also if Blessed Joseph of Cupertino has been canonized, and anything else that it behooves us poor solitaries to know. We are out of the world and it has been a year since I have heard either from you or from the college. If opportunity offers, I beseech you to send us wax candles for the altar, and the incense of which I wrote you that we stood in need. We are now sailing out of the harbor and one of the *San Carlos* boats will take this letter ashore, when it will be transmitted by a courier who is to leave San Diego tomorrow.

Junípero Serra

April 16, 1770

It is hard for us in our day of telephones, cables, wireless, radio and all our means of intercommunication to realize what mission work meant before these came. A great task did not exclude homesickness, and in this letter we can read how Father Junípero longed for news.

He had forgotten the incense, so Father Palou tells in the life of Father Serra that he wrote after his death. To leave one's possessions behind is a minor disaster now; it was a major one in Father Serra's day.

Still his depression never lasted long and he was soon making friends with the rough sailors, with the bluff captain and everyone on board. The rest did his lame leg good, though it was far from the much-desired healing. Father Serra ignored it as far as he could.

The short voyage proved a long one. They had fair weather and were not far from the coast, but adverse winds and exasperating, unseasonable calms kept the sails flapping aimlessly for days on end. It took seven weeks to make the short run, and Captain Portolá beat them to the port.

It was an easy expedition this time. He made his way directly over the trail by which they had stumbled back to the refuge of San Diego. Here, in the springtime, the way was far easier. They had an abundance of food, and by easy stages reached the neighborhood of the three crosses he had erected on three different headlands as a guide to the ships at sea.

They reached one at last. When he and Fages halted beside it they saw strings of decayed food placed before it and hung upon the arms. A row of arrows upside down spoke of peace. The Indians had recognized the white man's work. Evidently they considered it a possible god to be treated with respect and propitiated.

None of them were visible as Portolá, Fages and Costanso stood looking at it, while the rest of the party rested or wandered about. Doubtless black eyes were watching from the bushes and the trees and wondering what it all meant.

A sudden shout startled them. A man came running up and saluted.

"My comandante," he cried excitedly. "Look yonder. There is Vizcaíno's oak. Close on the shore it is lapped by the waves but with the remnants of the altar beneath it."

They turned incredulously. Another shout reached them. "The harbor, the harbor, Monterey!" another man was shouting.

The three officers ran over at full speed. Yes, there it was, lost Monterey. They had been within sight of it when they erected the cross. How could he have been so blind? Portolá thought.

There it was. The oval bay of Monterey lay at their feet. Seals were leaping and playing as they had done when Vizcaíno came. And there was the tree and the little ravine with a stream of clear water rippling through it—all that he had described. The three men knelt to drink the water as Vizcaíno had done before them, and then they looked about them marveling at the beauty of the place. Spring was at its loveliest in early May; this was indeed a paradise of God. The explorers reveled in its beauty. Then Portolá gathered them together in a formal ceremony. He took possession of the place in the name of Charles III, king of Spain and of these far lands, declaring that Monterey was the territory of Spain. A rattle of musketry followed his words.

They waited eight days for the *San Antonio*, lighting their friendly watch fires on the headlands to act as a guide. Which was the more joyous group, the men crowding the deck of the brave ship or those watching her eagerly as she came to her anchorage? The first boat was lowered and at its prow stood the slender figure they knew so well. Father Junípero had reached the place he had sought so persistently.

The finding of Monterey meant that California was Spain's, and there would be no more talk now of giving up, of bringing the Franciscans home.

Under Vizcaíno's oak an altar was swiftly erected. Upon it was placed a statue of our Lady holding the Child. Two bells swung above it, and as they pealed forth the pioneers knelt, singing the *Veni Creator* and the *Te Deum* with all their hearts.

Father Serra sang the Mass and dedicated the mission to San Carlos Borromeo and then sprinkled holy water on the beach "to put to flight the powers of evil," as he wrote later. He blessed the standards of Leon and Castile.

Once they were unfurled and saluted, Portolá dug out a small piece of turf, unearthed a stone or two and flung them as far as he could, thus dispossessing all other claimants to the land. Spain had made good at last; the Sacred Expedition had ended.

Councils were held. Portolá had accomplished his objective. He could go home with honor to receive his reward. Costanso would accompany him and Fages would remain in command. The *San Antonio* would put to sea as soon as possible.

Father Serra did not bother with the council. He and Father Crespi went exploring on their own account. A mission washed by the high tide would be of little use, and there were mistakes which had been made at San Diego that must be avoided here. They came back at sunset—happy. They had found the place they desired.

It was on a little river which they had named the Carmel and there they would place the mission. The cross could be erected at once. The barracks for the soldiers and the mission could be separated. There were many disadvantages in having them together.

Portolá did not argue. He was leaving at once. A courier, José Velásquez, was sent ahead, and a few days later the *San Antonio* sailed out of the harbor with flying flags. On August 10, 1770, Portolá arrived home. The acquisition of California was formally announced, all the bells were rung and Gálvez the viceroy and Portolá were the heroes of the day, acclaimed by the throngs that lined the streets hung with flags and banners.

It was a great day. No one thought then of the real hero, the Franciscan friar whose dauntless courage had made the expedition the success it was, instead of the failure it had so nearly become. It did not occur to anyone that the real hero was in Monterey. Nor did it occur to the hero himself as he watched the darkness fall over a lonely earth and a lonelier sea. But he was not lonely any more. God was with him and what else could he ask? Humbly he gave his thanks to the Lord who had guided him to this place where he could begin the great work of his life.

Monterey would be his home. He would have many weary

journeys up and down the coast and one exhausting one to Mexico, but always home would be here in the place he loved best on earth.

Soon there would be the adobe church, the huts and school. Later, Indian farmers would come and perhaps colonists as well.

Just now there was a beach of dazzling whiteness, a shaded river—and the blue Pacific as far as the eye could reach. This was the scene of his lifework, and here were his spiritual children whom he loved so well. Junípero Serra asked for nothing more.

VII. *The Building of the Missions*

CAPTAIN FAGES was no easy person to work with, Father Serra soon discovered. He was apt to regard all suggestions as unwarranted interference with his authority. It required tact, unlimited self-control and—what Father Serra could ill spare —time to get anything done.

But one thing had been accomplished—the division between the mission and the fort, which later might expand into a regular colony. Out on the Carmel River the trees were felled and the logs cut to start the church and the mission buildings. Once the work was really in hand, Father Serra went exploring on his own account.

Twenty-six leagues from San Carlos he discovered a place for another mission which he named San Antonio. There the Indians came at the ringing of the bell and knelt quietly during the first Mass. A gentle tribe and friendly, conditions were right here.

Back in San Carlos he found his workers had taken a holiday, so that it was almost Christmas before the buildings were completed.

But there was joy amid the difficulties. The *San Antonio* came in with ten friars and the promise of more to follow. There, too, with them were the longed for candles and incense and the bells for new missions. The letters came also and the news that the new Pope was indeed the Franciscan Ganganelli and that he had taken the title of Clement XIV.

Father Serra loved his bells. He had carried three across the desert, and next to the cross which symbolized the foundation of each mission he built a rough bell tower, generally for one bell alone, and that bell he rang himself whenever possible. "Come, come, and learn of Jesus Christ," each bell meant to him.

The bells did attract the Indians. As they heard the new sound coming over the hills, they came to the mission, peeping from behind bushes and rocks at first. Each day they returned and came a little nearer, gradually losing their fears entirely.

Two of the San Diego friars would have to go home, Father Serra decided. They had been ill and were weary and so he made arrangements for them to sail back on the *San Antonio*.

Young Father Jaime, whose love of Indians was almost as great as Father Serra's own, would become the head at San Diego with Father Dumetz.

The mission was really growing, for enough of the Indians understood some Spanish to interpret to the others. Father

Serra left Father Jaime to organize San Diego while he started other missions himself.

Of them all, San Antonio made the greatest and the fastest progress, while next to it was San Carlos at Monterey. The difficulties which they had all encountered at San Diego were nonexistent here. The crops were growing and the Indians—though not hard workers—were interested in them. Trees, shrubs and seeds of all kinds were coming in now from Mexico, for boats came and went with some regularity, while by land a trail had been made to Lower California where the road to Mexico City began.

The mission of San Gabriel proved in its founding to be as difficult a problem as that of San Diego. There the Indians were definitely unfriendly and for more than two years there were no conversions. Moreover, Captain Fages raised endless objections to the foundations, and with unfriendly tribes around it was necessary to have a Spanish barracks and a strong guard for a time. The soldiers did not get along with the Indians and Father Serra wrote sadly "that the San Gabriel tribes were not to be trusted," though "Thank God," he added, "at our other missions they become more trustworthy every day."

"They might all be Christians now were it not for the slowness with which we learn each other's tongues," he told Father Palou. "Only at San Diego has the difficulty been fully mastered. See to it that the new missionaries that you send us come well provided with patience, charity and good temper, for they will find themselves rich in tribulations. But where can the laboring ox go that the plow will not be heavy to drag? And unless he drags it, how can the seed be sown?"

Father Serra did not give up. His plan was a chain of missions from San Francisco to the channel of Santa Barbara. San Diego, San Carlos, San Francisco and Santa Barbara he planned to make "mother missions," with the others depending upon them.

"These four missions will stand in great cities some day," he said to Captain Fages more than once.

All seemed to be going well. Though Captain Fages had no belief in cities to come, he was under obligation to Father Serra. His mismanagement had caused a mutiny of one third of his force.

The situation had been both serious and ridiculous. To go out and fight the mutineers would only diminish the force at home, if indeed the soldiers would consent to fight their companions. It was rather like a sitdown strike and Captain Fages felt helpless.

He turned to Father Serra in his perplexity. Father Serra went after the mutineers.

"No, I am not going to take a guard," he told Captain Fages. "These men have not hurt anyone yet and they are not likely to begin with me."

Just what his reception was he never told. But he stayed with them and when the time was right set forth his arguments. These were clearly thought out. If the mutineers arrived home at all—with the difficulties of obtaining food by the way —they would find themselves in serious trouble with the authorities. Surely it would be wiser to use a little common sense and accept the terms that Captain Fages offered.

They listened and Captain Fages kept his word. On their

return, they found their hours of guard duty lightened, their abodes made more comfortable and the food divided fairly. They were grateful to Father Serra and so was the captain. San Gabriel was let alone and no opposition was made to the founding of San Juan Capistrano.

No one had any suspicion of the danger that was creeping slowly but surely upon San Diego. No one realized that black treachery was at work along the Colorado and in the hills.

There seemed to be no need for apprehension. Some four hundred baptisms had taken place, marriages had been solemnized and daily classes of instruction were carried on.

The crops had been harvested. Five years of labor was yielding abundant fruit and there was nothing to disturb the quiet peace of the place.

Father Dumetz had been replaced by Father Fuster, but it was gentle Father Luis Jaime who was the ruling spirit of the place. There was also a guard of three soldiers, two young boys, a son and a nephew of Lieutenant Ortega's, who had been left under Father Fuster's care, together with two blacksmiths and a carpenter. This formed the white population in 1775.

Father Jaime's heart was glad that fall as they harvested the crops, for two Yuma Indians appeared suddenly and asked for instruction and baptism. They had come a long way. The Yumas were all along the Colorado River and these two men came from one of the Yuma tribes far up toward the source.

They were intelligent; they spoke a little Spanish and seemed interested and earnest.

Father Fuster and Corporal Rocha watched them rather

closely. They were such silent men and their rather stolid faces gave little clue to their thoughts. One day they disappeared.

"The Yuma Indians have gone," Father Fuster reported to Father Jaime.

Father Jaime looked sad. He had been building great hopes on these new converts. "Perhaps they will come back," he said hopefully, but the days passed into weeks and nothing more was heard of them.

The Christian Indians knew nothing about them. Not a single warning reached any of the white men that danger was near. It was a time when few visits were made to the outlying villages, for the pastures were being extended and fenced. Small houses were being prepared for certain of the Christian families who wished to live at the mission.

"We shall have a ranch here next year," Father Jaime said happily.

The guards and the mission had been separated now for several years. As there had been no trouble since the first raid, no stockade had been built about the barracks.

The two Yumas had come to spy and now they were going up and down among the pagan tribes spreading the tale that the palefaces were planning to enslave all the Indians.

They were clever enough not to go to the Christians, but they sought the chiefs and impressed them. Plans were made very carefully. Indians crept to the appointed meeting places by ones and twos; the leaders held their councils in the shelter of the woods.

They had to wait for all the Yumas and when that powerful tribe arrived it was in full strength. There was a difference of opinion among the leaders as to what should be done—whether the missions should all be attacked at once or whether San Diego should be conquered and destroyed first.

The second plan won the approval of the plotters.

All was quiet in the mission that night of November fourth. All had been as usual. The busy workers had gathered in the mission chapel for evening prayer, had received their blessing and sought their villages. The two Ortega boys scampered up the hill to the monastery where their room was close to that of Father Fuster. Father Jaime was a little late. The carpenter was ill and he had had to go down to the barracks to minister to him.

The stars were out in the deep blue of the sky as he paused for a prayer at the cross. Then quietly he made his way to his own resting place.

An hour later, the Indians broke into the sleeping mission. Over the hills they came, a horde of painted warriors. They broke into the church, plundered it of its statues, its stations and the ornaments that had been fashioned with such loving toil. They stole the vestments, the albs, the surplices and the stoles.

Once the treasures were borne away, pandemonium broke loose. Casting their burning arrows on the roof of the church they set it on fire. In the light of the flames they danced their war dance and made the place hideous with war whoops and yells.

The mission woke. Father Jaime went out to face them with his usual greeting. They rushed upon him at once.

Father Fuster acted quickly. With the two boys he raced down to the barracks, where a fight was already in progress.

What hope could there be for any of them with this horde of half-crazed, bloodthirsty savages?

Urselino the carpenter had been the first to fall. He had staggered to the door and had fallen pierced with arrows.

"Indian, you have killed me, may God forgive you," he cried as he fell. José Komero tried to defend the entrance but, sorely wounded, fled with the other blacksmith to the small place of refuge next door where a stand was being made. There Father Fuster and the boys joined the defenders.

How they held out seems like a miracle. The barracks next door were ablaze. The sparks threatened their own small shelter. Father Fuster sat on the bag of gunpowder and wrapped his habit about it lest it should take fire. Nobody knew where Father Jaime was.

Corporal Rocha was the hero of the fight. He was the best shot and he fired continuously while the others loaded the guns. His unerring aim stopped the battle in the dawn. Even the Yuma Indians respected the white man's guns, and this particular gun was the worst they had encountered. Little by little they gave way. Soon the war whoops died down. They gathered up their dead and wounded and carried them as swiftly as they could to the hills.

When they were gone the defenders turned their attention to fighting the fire in their own small fort. The sun was high before they dared venture out of its shelter to hunt for Father Jaime and to see what was left.

The ruin was complete. The only building left was their own and that had a charred roof and walls.

The Christian Indians had fled, too. There was nothing left. And where was Father Jaime? The boys said that he had gone out fearlessly among the savages dancing and howling around the burning church.

"Love God, my children," they had heard him say, the greeting he always gave to his Indians.

Perhaps he was safe, they told each other. The Indians all loved Father Jaime. He had cared for them in sickness and in health. He had gone with his loving greeting in and out of their villages. He had brought aid to their sick; he had gathered their children in his arms.

Perhaps he was a prisoner; perhaps he had won them after all.

The search started and hope rose high. Then one of the searchers uttered a cry of dismay. In the brook they found the gentle leader. He had been dragged there, tortured and slain, his mutilated body recognizable only by its habit and his white skin. The first martyr of the missions had given his life for the Indians he loved.

"None of us doubt that he shed his innocent blood joyfully to water the vineyard in which he had toiled or that such an irrigation will give ripe fruit in converting the rest of the heathen," they wrote to Father Serra.

The survivors were wounded and burned, but they made litters upon which they laid the body of the carpenter and that of Father Jaime. There on the shore they buried them and sang their requiem close by San Diego Bay.

It was a month before Father Serra got the news. "The blood of the martyrs is the seed of the Church," he said amid his tears. God be thanked that the soil is watered and the real work can begin."

His next act was to write to the viceroy and tell him that

the Franciscans were not disheartened and that the mission would be rebuilt, though there might be delay in doing so. But the most important thing was to deal mercifully with the Indians themselves. Father Serra begged His Excellency to show pity toward the ignorant. Here was the chance for the white men to win the Indians, here was the opportunity to show that they had not come to supplant but to plant; not to destroy customs but to show mercy and truth.

Once the letter was dispatched, Father Serra hastened to San Diego where trouble in plenty awaited him. A discouraged mission was bad enough, but worse still were three fiery, angry Spanish commanders, eager to act and to take vengeance. Anza was for an Indian war at once; Ortega wanted to wipe out the Yumas, while Rivera with his usual impetuosity was raiding the Indian villages, arresting chiefs and warriors. All they were accomplishing was to arouse hostility anew.

On top of everything else, Rivera violated the law of sanctuary. An Indian crept back in penitence and took refuge in the church. Rivera demanded his instant surrender, and when it was refused he declared a ruin was not a church and went in and seized the fugitive.

"Protest away, Reverend Father," he said mockingly to Father Vincent. "I have the man."

Father Vincent did protest and sent word that Rivera and all concerned in the matter were excommunicated. Moreover, when Rivera ventured to church next Sunday he was ordered out.

Anza and Ortega did not approve of Rivera's actions. "He will bring all the Indians upon us," they grumbled. "But we must hang the chiefs."

Matters looked dark indeed. Father Serra managed to get a delay until word should come from the viceroy and then found that the delay was also to involve himself. He had started rebuilding but now Rivera withdrew all the troops on the pretext that the Indians were planning a new attack.

There was no truth in the rumor but Rivera was determined to have his way. So there was nothing to do but wait for word from the viceroy.

Junípero Serra had to learn patience in the hard school of experience. It was not the poverty, the difficulties and the hard work that troubled him, nor his constant pain; it was the long hours when day after day, week after week he had to wait and watch for letters and orders while the work was at a standstill.

Patience to him was not a natural virtue. The boy Miguel José had made his way into the novitiate by sheer force of will; the young friar had kept up his demand for missions in the face of opposition. The young priest had found no excuses for the people of Mexico City and their frivolous ways. His determined haste to walk through dangerous jungles to Mexico City had brought disaster upon himself.

Now he was learning. Though he was handicapped on all sides in the rebuilding of San Diego, there were still Indians to teach and it was one of them who brought him good news at last.

"Corporal Carrillo is on his way to San Diego, sent by the viceroy himself with a squad of soldiers ample for protection."

The corporal came in a few days later and brought with him the orders that must be obeyed—in a letter from the viceroy himself.

In view of the Christian sentiments to which Your Reverence gives expression, and inasmuch as you incline to believe that it would be more expedient to think of attracting the rebel Indians rather than chastise them, I have so directed. On this same date I am writing orders to Comandante Don Fernando de Rivera that he should act accordingly and bear in mind that this is the most suitable way to pacify and tranquilize the minds of the people.

The orders were explicit. All the natives concerned in the attack were to be pardoned. The man taken from the sanctuary of the church was to be released and an apology made to Father Serra. The new force was to guard San Diego, but Rivera was to assign suitable guards to all the missions, including the one in process of foundation, San Juan Capistrano.

Rivera could not override these directions.

It was a complete victory for the missions. "I doubt not that the suspension of the work of the restoration of the destroyed mission of San Diego must have given Your Reverence much pain," the viceroy wrote to Father Serra on Christmas Day. "The hearing of it has displeased me, and much more so for the frivolous reasons which brought it about."

A few weeks later, Rivera was recalled to Mexico and Felipe Neve was appointed as comandante and governor for Upper California.

That Governor Neve was a complete contrast to the impetuous Rivera and the irascible but kindly Portolá, Father Serra was soon to discover. He was a man of limited ideas and he clung to them tenaciously. He did not approve of Franciscans or of the plans of the missions. Worse still, he did not like Father Serra.

"Governor Neve is no friend to you, my father," Father Juan Crespi said one day to Father Serra. "Nor does he have any particular liking for the missions and the mission ways," he added.

Father Serra sat silent for some moments. He was always slow to criticize anyone. "The governor is new to this work of ours as well as to California, Juan," he answered at last. "We must try to make a friend of him. For the missions we do not need to be apprehensive. The governor has strict orders to consult with the viceroy and to propose whatever he considers expedient and necessary to make the establishments happy. He has been commanded to act in accord with me. The worst setback that we have at present is that we have neither the people nor the materials for the founding of the missions along the channel of Santa Barbara and those foundations will have to be postponed until later."

He went into the house and Father Juan looked after him. He knew what a bitter disappointment this postponement was to Father Serra. Santa Barbara would be the completion of his plan; it would be another port and, most important of all, it was surrounded by Indian tribes. There were souls to be won.

For a little while things seemed to go well. Help came. Cattle, sheep, mules and other livestock were brought in by hundreds across the desert. The *San Antonio* made swift voyages and came in bearing provisions and building materials.

Father Serra had proved right about the Indians. The return

of their doomed chiefs had brought back their confidence, and once the news spread that it was the "old father" who had pleaded for the chiefs, the Indians flocked to the missions.

They would walk miles to see Father Serra and to listen to his words. They were willing now to accept his invitation to live near the missions, to inhabit the cottages which they helped to build and to take up land for themselves as well as work with the missionaries. Conversions could be numbered by the thousands at last, and at each mission teaching of every kind went on.

But Governor Neve could not be won. He held to his distrust, and the prosperity of the missions seemed to annoy him. In important matters the governor was obliged to follow the orders of the viceroy; in small ones and in little details he proved an obstructionist.

Father Serra yielded in lesser things, but in the affairs and the care of Indians he was adamant. They were to be free. They were to be properly paid and properly housed. Any effort to enslave or ill-treat them roused his indignation and he would carry the matter to the viceroy as soon as possible.

There was much to do at all times and worries enough in the doing to discourage all but the bravest. A crop failed, difficulties arose, there was need for more help at every mission—and if there had been nothing else Santa Clara would have kept one man busy. Flood followed a fire and made half the mission uninhabitable; an earthquake shook down the rising walls. The Indians were unfriendly and the work discouragingly slow. If the friars had believed in luck they would have said that Santa Clara had none.

Anyone less determined than Father Serra would have given

up. That was not his way and he won out at last with his line of nine missions, all different and all doing God's work.

San Francisco, where already foreign ships were coming in to trade or to shelter in the harbor . . . San Luis Obispo with its orchards and wealth of olive trees . . . San Diego with flocks and herds and with San Antonio and San Carlos close to it in importance and progress . . . these gladdened Father Serra's heart. Perhaps the most beautiful of all was San Juan Capistrano with its flowers, its mighty trees, its vines and the heavy harvests of grapes. San Gabriel, San Buenaventura and even Santa Clara all had a work of their own.

"Perhaps Father Junípero will be able to rest a little now," the friars told each other hopefully as Father Serra returned to San Carlos. "All is well now."

VIII. *The Growth of the Missions*

"THE churches and the schools are the center of our missions, my brothers," Father Serra said. "Our own monasteries can wait; we can get along with what we have, but the churches and schools must be erected properly and of lasting material, for we build for the future."

He was not talking to the Spanish authorities now, but to those who shared his responsibilities, the Father Guardians of the missions who came together at San Carlos at Carmel-by-the-Sea for rest, refreshment and counsel.

Some of them had doubted Father Serra's wisdom when at Monterey he had not built San Carlos close to the barracks. He had separated the mission at once, seeking carefully until he had found this quiet spot on the Carmel River at a considerable distance from the place the military authorities had chosen.

"Is it safe?" some of them had asked. "You do not know the Indians of Monterey, my father."

"We did not come to California to avoid risks," Father Serra had answered. "What we came to do was to win Indians and *that* we cannot do on top of a barracks."

Today the visitors saw the outcome of the plan. Down out of sight—though not out of sound—was the fort, surrounded by barracks and small houses for the carpenters, blacksmiths and other craftsmen. Innumerable small huts had been erected for the muleteers, the servants and the Indians brought from Mexico.

"Already the settlement is growing," Father Crespi told the visitors. "The *San Antonio* and other ships make this their first port and each boat brings new arrivals for the settlement. Here we are alone. The Indians come to us and we can train them as we will."

Today everyone was willing to follow Father Serra's way. All the missions were outside the settlement and the plan now was to spread out, to reclaim land and make the missions to some extent self-supporting.

No one put in a plea for new monastic quarters. Though personal comforts were reduced to a minimum and the dwellings of the friars were still the flimsy shacks first erected, everyone knew that the poorest hut and the least convenient was Father Serra's own. They knew that he would always lead the way himself.

Father Serra was speaking gravely now. He had something very new to put before these men, something that called for sacrifice. Many of them had been sent from Lower California from monasteries they loved to do this pioneer work.

"My chief reason for this meeting is to tell you of a sacrifice that we have to make as an order," he said quietly. "We are undermanned and the work is growing. We count our converts by thousands now, thank God. The time has come when the children must be taught, when homes for the Indians must be built, when the Christians among them must be invited to live on the mission lands, to help us as they can but mainly to learn the Christian way of living, and to have their own lands and crops so that poverty will not make them wander away. All this is of the utmost importance and to do this we must have help. One or two fathers cannot develop a whole mission."

"But the College of San Fernando sent word that they could send no more missionaries at present," Father Vincent said.

"God has opened a way for us if we will accept it," Father Serra answered. "The Dominican Friars are able to take over the missions of Lower California and we have approached the authorities at San Fernando and also Viceroy Bucarelli for permission to arrange this. The plan has met with approval but the final decision is to rest with us. The coming of the Dominicans would release missionaries for us. Shall we say yes or no?"

There was no answer at first. It was a weighty question. Then Father Crespi spoke.

"God has called us to the missions here; God has blessed them," he said. "Surely He wants them to go on. And He has shown us the way."

"Say yes, Father Junípero," was the unanimous decision.

Father Serra watched his guests depart the next day. How good God was to send him helpers such as these, he thought.

He stood there smiling as he watched the busy mission that was his own. The pile of stone for the church was growing, though the Indians were slow workers. Some of the younger men were plowing and a group of older ones were gathered about Father Crespi as he talked to them of the things of God.

Over at one corner, Indian women were cooking over a wood fire, making their chia seed porridge and acorn bread. Others were fashioning the tamales that even the Spaniards liked. They were about the shape and size of an orange, black and a little greasy, flavored with almonds.

It was not hard to teach the women, Father Serra mused. They were eager to learn—and the young married men were not too difficult. But something would have to be planned for the older lads who abhorred school and who spent their time in idleness and mischief. There must be something that they would like. Just now Father Serra did not know what.

The children were Father Serra's closest friends. They were forlorn little things, very much neglected till they were old enough to be of some use. Father Serra had been horrified when he found that the chiefs were willing to give the children away, not only the girls but boys, too, in exchange for pieces of cloth and old iron hoops. A battered hat was worth a lad of eleven.

Father Serra had gone to the rescue and now every mission had its school which rang with the laughter of little boys who romped and raced, who picked up the Spanish tongue with ease and responded loyally to that of which they had so little—love.

As soon as Father Serra came in sight they ran to him, climbing all over him and settling down at his feet while he told them stories or listened to their tales. They loved the touch of his hand in blessing upon their heads, and the most coveted of honors was to serve his Mass.

"They are our hope," Father Serra would say when a new young father came to him in despair because the class of small boys had suddenly vanished out of the window and departed. "They probably saw a squirrel or a bird. They will come back, my son. Be patient."

Yes, little by little, things were growing. It had not been easy to teach the Indians better ways of living. "Why build a house of adobe?" one would ask. "It would have to be cleaned from time to time. The easiest way to clean a shack roofed with boughs was to burn it down and start afresh. Nor was there need to hurry about rebuilding. The summer nights were comfortable out of doors.

Only the rule that proper houses must be built on the mission lands or mission grants made any Indian consent to such waste of time and energy. But now some wanted to be with the fathers and had made a beginning.

It was some weeks later when he visited San Diego that Father Serra solved the problem of employment for the older lads. The flocks and herds of the mission had grown. Now the problem was how to look after them.

"We will make our own *vaqueros* or cowboys," Father Serra decided.

There was an abundance of horses. Wild herds roamed the valleys and the plains in such numbers that they were frequently a menace to the home farms and ranches, for in drought they invaded the pastures. Some of these were poor stock but there were good bands among them, mares and stallions that had drifted off from the expeditions and had inhabited some secluded place.

Riding was a new idea to the California Indians. They liked horse meat—and the herds would have been hunted down if they had not found it almost impossible to catch up with them. It took time and patience to teach them new ideas on the subject.

Father Serra chose his older lads carefully. It was a coveted honor to be enrolled in the class of the *vaqueros* and meant that there were tests to be made. A lad must be honest, fearless and willing to obey and learn before he could have the opportunity.

The enrolled boy received a blanket, a new loincloth and a serge blouse.

He had much to study and many a hard tumble before he was allowed to ride the range. Next he had to make a lasso, a task not too difficult for him, and to learn to coil it and throw it with accuracy. He was taught to brand animals and herd them. Only then could he join the others in hunting the wild horses and bringing them in to tame.

To blindfold and saddle a wild horse and then keep a seat on the back of the bucking, rearing creature was a hard task, but still more astonishing was the gentling, the stroking of neck and throat, then talking to the frightened pony till he knew his master.

"We have found the way, my sons," Father Serra would say when he visited his missions and saw the pastures where the cattle grazed with the Indian lads caring for them.

Father Serra's advice was sought in every mission. Though the others were no mean farmers, there were few who could tell so quickly when rotation was needed or what was ailing a poor harvest. He insisted on good cattle, sheep, mules and horses. The idea held by those at home in regard to pioneers that "anything would do for Upper California," met with no support from him.

His letters were insistent and he could "pester" if his demands were ignored. It was nothing for himself, always for someone else—and so the wealth of the missions grew.

It was not easy to be a good herdsman. There were real dangers surrounding the animals. The grizzly bear was a formidable antagonist and would come creeping down to carry off sheep and cattle if the herdsmen were not alert. Still more to be dreaded was the snarling puma with its sudden spring on cattle and men alike. The bobcat and the coyote took heavy toll at first till the Indians learned that the lasso was a weapon which could be cast and used to drag the snarling, fighting wild beasts out of harm's way.

"To make herdsmen of these Indians is pure folly," the soldiers and their comandantes would grumble. "They are worthless, useless, lazy and also liars."

Sometimes it seemed as if they were right. To have so many calves and good beef cattle at one's disposal in the far pastures, near the home which was so poor and where one's own people lived from hand to mouth, was a sore temptation and one which often proved irresistible. There were unauthorized feasts in the villages at first, and the puma and the bear also kept high festival while the herdsman joined the family party. The friars found that they must count every animal themselves when they returned home.

It was not Father Serra but one of the other friars who

solved the problem. His solution was spoken of far and wide. There was a young Indian in the San Diego Mission who was most capable and alert, an excellent rider and unafraid. Wherever a horse would take him he would go, and onlookers held their breath as they watched him leap the streams and the crevasses which no one else would attempt.

He fought pumas and bears valiantly and successfully, though his adventures were apt to enlarge themselves in the telling. Altogether, he was considered an excellent *vaquero* until he got near his own territory.

Then they found that he came back with fewer calves each day, and it was a very depleted herd that came back in two months. Proof was sought for and secured.

The boy was very penitent. Also he was dismayed. His horse and all his equipment belonged to the mission. If he was dismissed for this behavior he would have to go back to tilling the land, a task that he abhorred.

He took himself to the Father Guardian and poured out the whole story of his sins. He was going to be better. He was going to be the most reliable of *vaqueros* after this. He would tell no lies; he would never take anything that was not his— ever again.

The Father Guardian viewed his penitence with an effort to keep a stern and forbidding face.

"I could send you right away from us for all this, my son," he said at last. "We have done it before. No, do not weep. We may be able to give you another chance. First, you must prove all this reformation. Go to the mission school tomorrow, and when you have learned to read and write you may come back to me and we will see."

"Not ride? Not go to the pastures? Not tend the cattle?" the penitent cried in dismay.

"If you want to do those things again and are really sorry for robbing us, go and learn," said the Father Guardian firmly.

"I will go," the boy said sadly and made his way to the mission school and introduced himself as a pupil to the Father Master, who received him without enthusiasm.

Six long weary weeks—and oh, how long they were!—as he toiled at a desk, making endless pothooks with a pen clamped in his hand like a dagger or a knife. He spent hours trying to discover why *A* was not *B* and what *C* had to do with the matter anyway. Intellectual work was never the outstanding gift of the *vaquero*.

It was a sadder, wiser and very forlorn Indian boy who sought the Father Guardian six weeks later. "I am nothing but a wild Indian," the boy said wearily. "Oh, Father, let me go back to the herds. I will be the most honest Indian you ever had. The pothooks look worse every day and *A* and *B* and *C* grow more confusing. I will never steal again—I will tell the truth, always, always."

The Father Guardian thought for a few minutes. "I will give you one more chance, my son," he said at last, trying not to laugh when the lad leaped into the air with a shout which resembled a war whoop.

"I suppose we had better keep that lad in the home pastures from now on," the young brother farmer said diffidently the next evening, but the Father Guardian shook his head.

"Send him everywhere and especially near his own people," he answered. "That lad will not steal again."

He did not, though it involved bitter misunderstandings

with his own family. In the years that followed he loved to tell the story of how the fathers had made him trustworthy.

The story of his punishment had a far-reaching effect. It roused laughter now and then, but a sorely tempted *vaquero* would think twice before he allowed himself or his friends to steal.

An hour or two in the stocks, even a day or so in prison might be worth while, but pothooks and *A* and *B* and *C*— most decidedly not.

They were a wild and fearless set, these *vaquero* lads, but the fathers won them. Father Serra and his friars understood them, and there were fewer and fewer complaints as the years went on. The Spanish soldiers eyed the cowboys with astonishment as they came in to own up frankly about something that had gone amiss—my own fault, Father—was generally the end of the report.

The way was not all sunshine. There were many failures and disappointments when long hours of toil seemed to have gone for nothing. The old people were difficult, dull and always unpredictable. Worst of all, they had a way of picking up their families and belongings and disappearing overnight to some new hunting ground.

It was small wonder that sometimes the friars grew weary and discouraged and begged to go home to Mexico City and the regular life there.

Discouragement was the hardest thing for Father Serra to understand. He could see good in the most worthless material. He never faltered on his way for pain, fatigue, unkindness and danger. It took long years for him to learn to be patient with weaker men, but from the time he became the head of the missions he managed to acquire sympathy with the discouraged and was quick to discover if the reason for depression was inability, illness or a real need of change and rest.

To all the friars, as well as to himself, the rule was the same. "No service is too great, no service is too small, if it helps to win Christ's people," said Father Serra.

The plans and the growth of the missions met with unkindness in one quarter. Governor Neve looked with suspicion upon Father Serra and all his work. He disapproved of *vaqueros*, of mission schools and ranches. Most of all, he resented the fact that Father Serra could win the confidence and love of the Indians.

Viceroy Bucarelli held the governor in check in graver matters so that he had to content himself with small hindrances and objections which delayed plans and often building. He managed to find endless excuses for not going forward with the foundations along the Santa Barbara Channel. He must wait for a ship or for a letter coming overland; the weather was not suitable; he had not enough soldiers for guards to new places. The excuses were endless.

Father Serra made few protests except where the Indians were concerned. At all times he protected them and in each case successfully.

For himself, Father Serra made no defense. He went quietly on his way working for his missions and the mission people. No service, as he said, was too small.

"What are you doing?" Father Crespi asked one afternoon as he came upon his superior sitting on a rock, a piece of cloth clutched in one hand and a needle with a very long thread in the other.

"I am sewing, my son," Father Serra answered. "At least, for my sins, I am trying to learn," he added ruefully.

"But why?" Father Crespi asked blankly.

"The women have to be taught and there is no one to teach them, Juan."

It would be interesting to know how that sewing class progressed, but beyond a brief comment that the Indian women did learn, no one has given any details. Probably they did much to teach themselves. For the "old father," they would always do their best.

The delays and hindrances continued, and at last Father Serra decided that the only way to settle matters was to talk with the viceroy himself.

There was no boat sailing for Mexico just then and so Father Serra decided to walk. He started on the long trail across the desert with one Indian lad. They took the Camino Real, following the golden mustard as they went. The two made good progress at first, but it was summertime and the heat soon became almost intolerable. They were obliged to rest part of the day and go on far into the night. Worst of all, the springs were very low and it was hard to find water. When they found a spring, low though it might be, they drank of it freely, unsuspicious of danger.

It took far longer than Father Serra had expected to reach the road to Mexico City. Such a walk was always an ordeal for him, but this time he was so utterly weary that at night he wondered if he could possibly reach his destination.

The Indian lad was tall and strong. He was used to the desert and the roughness of the way. He could run long distances like the rest of the Indian boys, but now he could hardly keep pace with Father Serra. At night he tossed restlessly and muttered in his own tongue, his hands as dry and hot as Father Serra's own.

It was not fatigue; it was the "great fever"—as the Mexicans called it—the dreaded typhoid that was upon them both.

The desert was behind them. Now there were wooded places, a good road and less heat, but there was nowhere to stop. The nearest place was the Mexican border and oh, how far away it seemed!

The two stumbled on, they hardly knew how, falling from time to time, but at last the border was reached and they knocked at the door of a Franciscan monastery.

The travelers were welcomed, cared for and carried to the infirmary where, in spite of all the nursing and skill, they slipped for days further and further down the valley of the shadow of death.

Ill as he was, Father Serra kept praying—not for his own recovery but for the lad's. The boy was young, he was needed and, worse yet, if he died here in a strange land they might say it was foul play.

Father Serra's prayers were answered, the prayer he had prayed and the one he had not. Slowly, oh, so slowly, the shadow moved backward as the crisis passed and strength came back. As soon as he could manage it—far sooner than his nurses approved—Father Serra set out for Mexico City, leaving the boy behind to get well. He arrived there weak and weary, a shadow of his old self.

It was a happy visit and for once a restful one. Friends crowded arounnd Father Junípero and, best of all, the viceroy was willing to give him unlimited time.

The two men talked long together, the viceroy's dark face alight with interest as Father Serra told of all that had happened. He was promised all the help that Don Bucarelli could give to him. Still more eager were the groups gathered about him in the evenings at the Franciscan College as he told the tale of California and the founding of each mission.

It was a sore disappointment to find that there were no bishops to send to California. Mexico was undermanned, too.

But there was help. By special license of the Holy Father at Rome, Father Serra was authorized to administer confirmation. The holy oils were given to him with a copy of the patent giving the permission and strict instructions as to the use to be made of the privilege.

With a glad heart he set sail for California, and once he reached San Carlos, he began his new work. Classes of instruction were started in all the missions and he went from one to another—confirming all those who were ready for the gift.

All seemed bright before him now. Small annoyances did not matter when he had this great work to do. With Don Bucarelli behind him, the new missions would soon be founded.

Late one night a messenger rode in bearing bad tidings—the loss of their protector and the onset of dark days for the missions. The viceroy was dead and until a successor was appointed Upper California was under the rule of Governor Neve!

IX. "That Friar"

"You may not confirm these Indians or anyone else. You have arrogated to yourself an office which does not pertain to you, Father Serra," Governor Neve said haughtily. "As usual, you have gone on your way without consulting the secular authorities which I represent. I utterly refuse permission for this or any other innovations that you may be contemplating."

Father Serra did not answer for a few moments. Though he had been sure the curt summons to come to the governor's headquarters meant some interference, he had not expected that Felipe Neve would endeavor to rule not only the missions but the Church. When he finally spoke it was with the quietness which his companion Father Crespi knew was necessary to keep back words of hot indignation.

"The shortage of clergy in Mexico is the reason that no bishop can be sent at present to Upper California, Your Excellency," he said. "I found that the authorities in Mexico were concerned about this and that they had obtained from Pope Clement himself the necessary *patente* to enable one of the friars to administer the Sacrament of Confirmation. By my own superiors and with the consent under his official seal of viceroy Bucarelli I was appointed. I was given a copy of the document together with full instructions concerning what I was to do—as well as being entrusted with the holy oils for the purpose. I can show you what I have, though I sent the *patente* to the Father Guardian of San Fernando at his request, in order that he might have the signature of the new viceroy added to it."

"I shall be content with nothing but the original brief," the governor retorted. "I do not trust copies in matters in which you are concerned, Father Junípero. In appealing to the viceroy, you have for once made a mistake. The arrangement has been made to divide responsibility for the New World lands, and it is the Comandante de Croix who has the supreme authority for California. I shall write and lay this matter before him as soon as may be."

"Then it is to the Comandante de Croix we are to appeal in matters of difficulty," Father Serra replied, and the governor bit his lip.

He had not meant Father Serra to know that fact just yet. What was there about this lame friar that made one tell him the things one had decided not to mention? the governor wondered.

"At any rate the confirmations cease at once," he announced with decision.

"The confirmations will cease," Father Serra agreed. "Some

of the old men and women may go to the heavenly country before they receive the gift. Our Lord can make it up to them; I know that He will. The hindrance is a matter that lies between Your Excellency and Christ Himself. I leave it there."

He rose and departed, followed by an angry Juan Crespi.

"How dared he insult you so, Father," the younger friar burst out. Father Serra's hand came down upon his clenched one.

"When men speak evil of you, rejoice and leap for joy," he paraphrased laughing. "The leaping is not in my power any more, but I can do the rejoicing, Juan. The governor is following his own conscience after his own fashion. It is not for us to judge. We do not matter, but for our Indians we must act. Find our swiftest runner while I write to Comandante de Croix. He is honest; he is interested in the missions and he is a friend."

Father Serra was not the only letter writer that afternoon. Governor Neve sat long over the missive that he was writing.

Father Junípero Serra says he sent his *patente* to the Father Guardian. I do not proceed and take possession of the mission or make a search for the papers, because it not being certain that he sent them away, he will with his unspeakable artifice and shrewdness have hid them and the result will be delay in the channel foundations, because these fathers would then not furnish the supplies which they have to contribute. If exasperated, there is no vexation which these religious, with immeasurable and incredible pride, will not attempt, since on four or more occasions my policy and moderation were not enough to turn them from the opposition with which they surreptitiously conspired against the government and its ordinances. At a more opportune time, certain measures may be taken, which for the present it has been judged necessary to postpone, in order to bring this Father President to a proper knowledge of the authority which he eludes, while he pretends to obey.

Signing his name, the governor laid down his pen, sanded the sheet before him and surveyed his letter with satisfaction. This was a masterpiece, he thought, which might, if fortune served, rid him of the one man who stood in his way.

To fight with Father Serra was difficult. How was one to get the upper hand of a man who went on his way, quietly held his own, never got excited, who listened with a calm face to tirades and, worst of all, made his opponent feel and look ridiculous.

"It is a thing unbearable that we should be at the mercy of an ignorant, lame old friar," he said as he sealed his letter.

"Hardly ignorant, Your Excellency," an underling ventured to remind him. "Father Junípero Serra is one of the learned men of our time. He could hold great office in Europe."

"I wish he had it," growled the governor. "However, he is going to obey me now. Send this letter off by special messenger."

Father Serra was obeying now. The blow had been a harder one than he allowed anyone to know. He was old and strength was failing him. There was so much to be done. While others rejoiced at the number of baptisms, Father Serra knew that unless those converts were established in the faith, the work would come to nothing. Delay was indeed hard to bear. He spent much time in prayer and vigil, telling no one of his grief.

It was not the matter of the confirmation alone. That would be settled easily enough by the authorities in Mexico City. It was a new plan of Governor Neve's that, if carried out, might ruin the missions. The governor was casting covetous eyes on the fields, the flocks and the herds of the missions. The friars needed no ranches. They could keep the spiritual side and keep to it strictly. The ranches, the fields, the flocks and the herds could be given to the white colonists he was planning to bring in, and the Indians could return to their villages and be governed by their own chiefs.

"The Indians are not ready to govern themselves as yet," Father Serra had told Felipe Neve. "As for the missions, we shall go on as we have always done until we get from our superiors the order to change our ways."

That was the crux of the whole matter, Father Serra knew, and it was for his missions as well as his Indians that he agonized in prayer.

Governor Neve had decided to leave Father Serra alone in this matter, but he was making plans for a colonization of his own type among the Yuma Indians on the Colorado River, which was outside Father Serra's jurisdiction.

Father Serra had given his warning. Such a plan was a dangerous one. The Yumas were a progressive and warlike tribe. Unless the white colonists were kept strictly in check, there might easily be a clash which would lead to an Indian war. If the Yumas arose, the trouble might spread to these more peaceful tribes on the coast.

Governor Neve had snorted derisively. An Indian was an

Indian, one of a savage people who could easily be controlled. Besides, this was none of Father Serra's business.

Father Serra said no more. Instead, he took his worries to the King of Kings. Then, with peace in his heart, he made the most of the waiting time.

The classes of preparation for confirmation could go on in every mission. And every friar was to make the utmost effort to make friends with the Indians scattered throughout the mountains and the valleys.

The waiting time was long. By sea or by land, the journey to Mexico was tedious and quite frequently the messengers proved irresponsible. One of them had left the very first mail for Father Serra in some monastery in Lower California, together with needed supplies for the church and mission.

All anyone could do was to wait and hope that the important reply of Comandante de Croix would be entrusted to a sure hand and that no misfortune would happen on the way.

It came at last—not to Father Serra but to Governor Neve. It was an answer that he did not expect.

"The Governor has nothing to do with the spiritual affairs of the missions," the comandante wrote curtly. "Father Serra's *patente* is in order and came directly from Rome. The papers are in the keeping of the Franciscan College where they should be. Father Serra is to be let alone and it is urgent that the channel foundations go forward as soon as possible."

Governor Neve was outraged. He had not expected anything like this but there was absolutely nothing he could do about it. He was obliged to obey. His letter to Father Serra was written with no enthusiasm whatever.

Under date of December 23 last, the comandante general informs me that he has been assured by testimony, which His Excellency the viceroy directed to him, that the Pontifical Brief, in virtue of which Your Reverence is granted the faculty to confirm, had received the pass of the Supreme Council of the Indies and of the captain general of Mexico, and that with this I should not prevent Your Reverence from administering the said Holy Sacrament. I inform Your Reverence of this so that you may use the said faculty in the new establishments as you judge expedient.

Reluctantly enough, he sent the letter off and said nothing about the new missions which he knew well were of the first importance to Father Serra. Father Palou says charitably in summing up the matter, "that it is not supposed that Governor Neve was influenced by malice, but rather that, lacking advisers, he acted as his judgment dictated."

Father Serra made no complaint or protest.

Bucarelli had been succeeded as viceroy by Martin de Majorga, but the division of authority under comandantes general brought trouble to California. The unwise plan of Governor Neve to restrict the missions to spiritual help to the Indians was not only considered but accepted. A new sort of colony was started on the Colorado River.

The question was money. Colonists were ready to come and Father Serra had urged their coming. Two colonies had been started at San Jose near the mission of Santa Clara and one at Los Angeles near San Gabriel. These colonies were separate from the missions except for spiritual help.

It was thought it would be cheaper to found secular colonies separate from the missions leaving the latter to make their own way. Later, something could be done about the mission lands but of that there were only rumors and whispers. No longer were the friars to go with the means of colonization, but they would be sent to found spiritual missions without money or authorization to make bargains with the Indians or to sign treaties or anything else.

Father Garcias and Father Diaz were appointed to lead a band of settlers to the Gila River where the Yumas were.

There were warnings enough. Father Garcias protested vigorously that it was impossible to found a mission as if the country around it were wholly civilized and Christian. Father Garcias knew the country and its inhabitants well, and he reiterated Father Serra's warning about the Yumas. Anza the great explorer added his experience and words but these, too, were brushed aside.

Father Garcias was advised not to go. He knew the danger only too well, but under obedience he went—with a clear-eyed knowledge of what was likely to befall him.

De Croix went on his way. He believed in the friars and had sense enough to realize the work that they had done. He admired Father Serra and had at once promised him protection and help.

"Your Reverence will find in me all that you desire for the advancement of our holy faith and the glory of religion. I beg your prayers and those of your religious for the happy issue of the important things committed to my care," he had written when he first took office.

"The Yumas would be all right," he and Governor Neve agreed. The chief was their friend and had announced his willingness to have a colony of Spaniards near him, for he

considered the Spaniards lords of the earth. The Yuma chief
went around boasting of his friendship with the white men,
and he believed implicitly all the promises that were made him.

Oh, yes, there was nothing to fear, and so the friars and the
colony were sent out empty handed to settle on land that,
after all, was Yuma land, on the river on which the Yumas depended for their crops, their fish and their water.

No arrangements could be made by the mission. All bargains
with the Indians meant gifts, and nothing was binding unless
these had been exchanged. No one had anything to give, and
the Yuma chief watched with greedy and disappointed eyes
the white men calmly settling themselves on his land.

He had expected gifts and large gifts and they were not
forthcoming. The settlers themselves had been chosen with
no care. Many of them were not white men but mulattoes and
Mexican Indians. They scorned the tribesmen among whom
they had settled and, worst of all, destroyed the corn crops,
the Indians' most precious possession. Starvation threatened the
Yumas, who had been one of the wealthiest of the western
tribes.

Protests were laughed at. Father Garcias tried his best to
help, but his hands were tied by lack of anything to give.

Rivera and his small body of men had the task of guarding
the place. He ruthlessly punished any aggression and made no
effort to set matters right. He had apparently forgotten—if
he ever knew—that the King of Spain had expressly forbidden
the stealing of any Indian lands, no matter how great the need
might be.

There was hardly a mistake that had not been made.
De Croix, Neve and Rivera all took it for granted that the river

Indians were the same type as those of San Diego and Monterey. Those Indians would have moved farther on, disgruntled perhaps, but harmless.

The Yumas were not nomads. They were men of the land and they loved it and their homes, which were real ones—not shacks of green boughs. Moreover, they were neither timid nor stupid nor lazy; they were fighters, as the friars well knew. The chief at this time was a man of great shrewdness and initiative, disguised by his apparent acceptance of promises and his delight in uniforms. He often made speeches to his people which the white men did not understand, and although the situation was not harmonious, not even Rivera realized that the chief was giving orders concerning a plan. Nor did anyone take alarm at the number of Indians who came day by day to the river. They belonged to the Yuma tribes or those closely allied to them and usually stayed a very short time. That the hills, the plains and the mountains had many Indians roaming around in them, the white men knew. However, they did not realize that the newcomers were all warriors and that no women or children accompanied them. The chief was clever. There were no council meetings, no war dances, no warpaint, no warning whatever.

The attack came with the suddenness of a thunderbolt. Everything had been as usual all day, and everyone in the colony went to bed soon after dusk. Rivera had set no guards.

At midnight the settlement woke to the sound of warwhoops—to find their fields and houses blazing while a horde of Indians, screaming like demons, went through the place killing every man with a wantonness that added to the hopelessness and terror.

No man was held prisoner. In vain, Palmas pleaded for Father Garcias when the Indians tried to kill them both. Not a man was spared, not even the friars—although the Yumas had counted them friends. Nor did their heroism affect the Yumas, as the friars moved among the wounded and the dying, striving to protect the women and children, praying beside the dead until they themselves fell.

Comandante Rivera and his men fought desperately, taking heavy toll of the savages, but to the last man they were slain. The morning sun rose on the wrecked settlement, on dead men lying beside the river, while the women and children were herded into groups and carried off into captivity.

They were not too badly treated, though they were divided among the Yumas as workers and slaves. The Indian women were usually kind to children, while the possibility of training white boys into Indian warriors was always attractive to the tribes. Most of them held firmly to the view that the white man's civilization and his wonderful possessions, especially his guns, were the result of powerful magic. White Indian men would have that magic, they reasoned, and therefore welcomed as captives the paleface boys.

A chief who could marry a white girl might win that magic for his sons, so girls were protected, too. The women could cook and spin and teach their captors many things.

It took time for the disaster to become known. One record says that a young ensign and his men marching to the place found it in ruins. He was attacked and met the fate of the others, but one man managed to get away and bring the news to Monterey.

It dazed them all at first. For Father Serra, there was the

grief of losing his sons and also the anxiety for the other missions as well.

Yumas, flushed with victory, might be coming toward them from any point—and Governor Neve's idea had been to reduce the guards of each place as much as possible.

The other missions were not attacked. Probably the reason was that the Indians remembered San Diego and what they had lost there. Also they would remember that when their chiefs were taken it was "the old white father" who had pleaded for them and had restored them to their people. An Indian's memory is as tenacious for a good deed as for a bad one.

Governor Neve and Comandante de Croix spared themselves self-reproach by a flame of anger against the Indians, whom they accused of treachery and apostasy, quite forgetting that by their own mismanagement lands had been stolen and the friars hampered in every way from teaching the pagan Indians.

Captain Fages was sent out to take vengeance, only to find that there were no Indians to fight—except when they decided to swoop unexpectedly on a group of his soldiers.

All he succeeded in doing was to ransom sixty-four women and children—so the Yumas were quite unharmed and the richer for his arrival. A second expedition ransomed ten more captives, secured some church vestments and sacred vessels and brought back the bodies of the four missionaries.

The third expedition was a little more successful. A battle took place, costly in lives on both sides and costlier still in the hate it engendered. A thousand horses were recovered, eighty-five Indians were taken prisoner and the seven remaining captives freed.

"The troops and settlers are well received by the Yumas," De Croix had written a few months before to the viceroy. "The results will doubtless be happy, for a union with the Spanish pueblos will foster the docility of the Indians and protect the communication with New California and make Sonora secure. The establishments will cost only the allowances made to each settler's family—only forty-seven pesos a year—and that to stop as soon as they are self-supporting. The banks of the Colorado will be covered with fields, cattle and towns of faithful vassals."

Bitter had been the cost of the economy. Lives and fields and flocks, orphaned children and widowed mothers, soldiers of Mexico and, worst of all, a heritage of distrust and hate were the payments that had been made. There was no hope of re-establishing the pueblos or of conciliating the Indians; the Colorado plan would have to be abandoned.

Father Serra grieved for all his sons, but Father Garcias was a sore loss indeed. Alone, this solitary friar, the only white man among savage tribes, had traversed two thousand miles of wilderness, opened up the trails that are now our great highways and had made maps and notes.

He knew only too well that the Yumas were only biding their time, but his warnings were unheeded and quietly he remained at his post to do what he could.

In spite of all the sorrow and confusion, the missions steadily grew. The Christian Indians now numbered thousands and the missions themselves were places of busy work.

Up and down among their people the friars went, and now

villages as well as mission schools rang to the sound of children's voices, while the miserable old shacks were slowly disappearing.

"But they sing as badly as ever," Father Crespi mourned from time to time. Certainly the Indians were no musicians, and their instruments—things that would clatter and clash—were never in harmony.

"But I suppose you will say as usual that it is their best noise," Father Crespi would say to Father Serra with a smile, comforting himself with preparing the dramatic representations at which their Indians excelled.

A small brown baby represented the Christ Child at Christmas and a Mother and St. Joseph watched over him, sometimes in the church itself and sometimes in a near-by cave. There were real shepherds to come and worship, and tall chiefs in gorgeous robes, representing the kings from the East, came to kneel with them. The *vaqueros*, the farmers, the fishermen —all came and all made their act of adoration and worship.

There were processions on the great feast days and high festival on the days dedicated to our Lady. Each morning at dawn the Indians crowded into the church to recite the morning devotion in praise of the Most Holy Sacrament, our Lady and her most pure and holy conception. In their own language the Indians recited the Creed, the Hail Mary, the Our Father, the Confiteor and their acts of faith, hope and charity, the Ten Commandments and all the great doctrines of the Christian religion.

At the end of the Mass, each one was called by name and came up and kissed the priest's hand and listened to any special word he might have to give.

In and out among them all went Father Serra, making his visitations for confirmation, going from San Carlos to San Francisco. The friars wondered how he could possibly walk, for the wound on his leg had spread halfway up now, and the authorities sent physicians to see what they could do.

It was little enough. "I have not time for this, my sons," Father Serra would say laughing. "It is nothing—it can be borne."

His friends looked after him in dismay as he started off—the leg had to revolt utterly before he would ride—and often the physicians wondered how he could take one step after another, not knowing the secret of Father Junípero Serra, the fact that he never had time to think about himself. There was so much work to be done.

X. *The End of the Way*

"Thanks be to God." Father Serra's worn face lighted up as he laid down the letter sent to him by Governor Neve. At last the authorities were moving and the summons to found the mission of San Buenaventura was here.

Doubtless it would mean the mission of Santa Barbara, too, the one that Father Serra had been planning for years. There was so much work to be done on the channel of Santa Barbara, and how he longed to do it!

The relations between Father Serra and the governor were better than they had been. Felipe Neve had found he needed Father Serra when the Yuma War broke out and the disaster on the Colorado River was known. If the coast Indians had joined the Yumas it might easily have meant the loss of all the Spanish settlements. The governor found that he needed the missions and—most of all—Father Junípero who went fearlessly from village to village making peace.

Governor Neve was grateful after his own fashion. He refrained from petty interference, though he still held to his idea that a colony should be a colony and a mission a mission.

Father Serra did not argue with him. Governor Neve would never see that a mission without the power to make treaties or to help a pagan people in sickness, need and poverty would make but little progress. The whole matter was in abeyance at present, for the white colonists were afraid of the Indians of Upper California.

The biggest problem was that of new missionaries who were unwilling to come because of the threat of these regulations. And many of those who had toiled and worked through the years were discouraged at the thought of depending upon a military post for aid and equipment. Even the two Father Guardians—Father Lasuen and Father Figuer—had begged to go home to Mexico.

Father Serra had had to cheer and encourage and persuade them to stay, turning to the task with all the faith and courage he had displayed when Portolá had wanted to give up.

"Is it worse to have an appetite with nothing to eat or to have much to eat and no appetite?" he asked the weary ones. "We have gone through the time when we had nothing, and now we have our missions, our spiritual blessings and our converts. It is not only the children and the young men and women now, we are winning the old people at last. Have we the right to complain? What we have to do in these missions is of great magnitude and I do not wonder at your anxieties. Do not imagine that we fail to do all that we can when we leave everything to God. He who sends or permits adversities provides as much patience as is necessary."

The fathers did not go. Instead, they took new courage from their leader and devoted themselves to the building up of the work.

But hearts were heavy at San Carlos, for the friars realized that Father Serra had suddenly grown old. They noticed it first when Father Juan Crespi died on New Year's Day of 1782.

Father Juan had come back from a tour of the missions, where he had gone as companion to Father Serra, who was confirming all who were ready for the sacrament. The illness came upon him almost at once and all the care and nursing were of no avail. The blow to Father Serra was a heavy one. Although he accepted the sorrow and made no outward sign of his grief, he was lonely now. More and more he had depended upon Father Crespi. Together they had built San Carlos; together they had shared anxieties and troubles; together they had journeyed to and fro. There was no one to take his place, though Father Palou had come to Upper California a year ago. His mission was too far away from San Carlos for him to be anything but an occasional counselor.

Father Serra had lost ground in the past months. Not only was the wound in his leg more troublesome, but he was no longer able to hide a still more serious trouble—a growth on his breast that caused breathlessness from time to time and then enveloped him in waves of such pain that he was obliged to rest.

He picked up the governor's letter now and called his household together to tell them the good news. Joy had given him new strength and he brushed aside the protests that were offered.

"Ought you to go?" they asked.

"God has called me. He will give me strength to do His will," was the answer.

The expedition for the channel of Santa Barbara started on Tuesday of Holy Week. It was a strange mixture: the governor, seventy soldiers and their families, some officers, many muleteers and Indian servants, together with Father Serra and one companion.

After the first night the governor was recalled. The Yumas were giving trouble again and Captain Fages needed advice. The expedition proceeded without him.

On Easter Day the mission of San Buenaventura was founded, Father Serra sang the Mass and preached on the Resurrection, his face aglow with happiness. This was a foundation different from all the others, for there was a large ranch of Christian Indians close by. The pagan tribe came to peep around corners until they felt confidence enough to come and make friends.

The next days were busy ones. The Indians helped build the mission, and two weeks later Father Serra went with the soldiers to the one which for so long had been the desire of his heart—Santa Barbara. He wrote of the mission to Father Lasuen.

On the Feast of the Patronage of St. Joseph, occurred the erection of the great cross and the blessing of the locality with Holy Mass and a sermon. It was the mission of Santa Barbara, Virgin and Martyr, on the land of Yannonlit. I was and am alone, and therefore, the Mass was a low Mass. In place of the *Te Deum*, we had the usual devotions. May God bless Santa Barbara. Amen.

God would bless this latest mission; of that Father Serra was confident, but he himself was not to see the buildings rise.

Two days later, Governor Neve caught up with the expedition.

"No," he declared obstinately. "You had no permission to found the mission of Santa Barbara, Father Junípero. No buildings will be erected here until the Praesidio is finished."

"That will take time," Father Serra said.

The governor looked uneasy. He knew he could not deceive Father Serra, who knew only too well that what the governor wanted was his own way, and that by making this delay he might be able to secure the kind of colony he desired and so cripple the mission. He did not want schools for the Indians or work for the *vaqueros*.

"Since Your Excellency is not going to found a mission, I am superfluous here," Father Serra told him. "I shall pass on to Monterey. From there I will send two fathers and in the meantime, lest so many people be without Holy Mass and anyone to minister to them, I will send one of the missionaries from San Juan Capistrano."

The governor made no effort to change the decision, and after a night spent for the most part in prayer beneath the cross Father Serra started on his way.

He will never see those buildings rise, the governor thought as he watched the frail figure start on the long journey alone. He was half inclined to call Father Serra back, but his own way was still his goal.

Father Serra was worn out when he reached San Carlos, and as he grew weaker every day he quietly faced the fact that for him life was ending.

He knew it himself and wrote Father Palou a long letter of instructions on the office of the president and the needs of the missions—"because the next thing you may receive concerning me may be the notice of my death. Recommend me to God."

They all knew that his nights were sleepless ones, often spent on a chair to ease his breathing. It was in those long watches and in the midst of his pain that he made his plans, and as usual he carried them out at once. There was one more thing to do.

"I am going to visit all the missions and confirm," he said to the household one morning and his laugh rang out as gaily as ever at their expressions of dismay. "You do not need to get so excited. God can bring me home if He so desires; if not, I shall die doing His work. What more can one ask?"

All they were able to win was the promise that he would go by sea instead of walking. "There will be doctors on board the ship," the friars whispered to each other. "He will have nothing to do. He may let them help him."

Little did they know their Father Serra. He found soldiers and sailors on board who had never been confirmed and he started his instructions at once.

The surgeons were allowed to look at him and they shook their heads over the chest and leg. "Let us take care of you," they urged him. "You must rest, not walk and work."

"I have no time just now for rest," Father Serra insisted. "I have work to do—and my leg and other ills have never stopped me yet. When we get back to San Carlos, well, then we will see."

He landed in San Francisco and from there made his way to all his loved missions. It was a happy visitation. There were children and men and women to be baptized, goodly classes of those ready for confirmation, and his old friends gathering about him as soon as the news of his arrival got abroad. Santa Clara was out of trouble for once, with a new church to be blessed, and there was his beloved San Gabriel whose silvery bells rang out a welcome to him.

> "And every note of every bell
> Sang Gabriel! Rang Gabriel!
> The tower that was built to tell
> Of Gabriel, Archangel!"

His joy overcame his pain and his face flushed and his eyes grew bright as he entered the church. People thought he was better then. But the friars knew. "When he prays and sings he is always strong. Nevertheless, he is dying," they told each other sadly.

Eager to greet him were Father Lasuen and Father Figuer. They wanted to tell him that their depression had passed. He talked long and happily with them. He saw them all—the men who were eager and enthusiastic, the lonely, the discouraged and the overworked.

"How well he understands!" That was what they all said or thought as they heard the stories of his journeyings. He had no blame for the homesick young friar, all alone in a mission whose Indian boys had comforted him with a gift of four small kittens which they put in his bed. The kittens frisked everywhere and followed their master wherever he went. Some of the brothers had been shocked at such childishness; Father Serra had laughed and understood. Good, too, he thought, the cure of an irascible old friar whose four serene cats sat in a row to welcome him and attended meals with their owner.

Father Serra loved all animals but he had no pets, although he was never too sick, too tired or too busy for the children. He talked to the children of the heavenly country to which he was bound, and they listened and understood.

"He says he is going home," they told each other wide eyed. "Our Lord wants him. The old father is going to die."

In each place as he left it he stood looking around him, saying farewell to the places he would never see again. He looked at the wide pastures, at the *vaqueros* riding with the herds. He watched the older men and women at their tasks and, last of all, he knelt at the foot of the cross which marked his work.

Then very quietly with a prayer on his lips he departed, walking with difficulty while dim eyes watched him.

He reached San Carlos at last and there—an ominous sign— he let the doctors have their way. Not that they could help— their rough surgery only added agony to his pain.

During sleepless nights and weary days he was lonely with a loneliness that was greater than any he had endured before. One day he managed to write a letter to Father Palou—demanding nothing but ending with a pathetic "If you could come! . . . but God's work must be done."

Three or four days later, as he sat in his bare little room the doorway was darkened by a tall figure, and Father Serra's tired eyes brightened and his face flushed with joy as Father Palou—his pupil, his companion and comrade and his dearest friend—came in and knelt beside him.

"I have come and I am staying," Father Palou said.

They went to the church and so strong was Father Serra's voice in the *Te Deum*, which was sung to give thanks for Father Palou's arrival, that hope sprang up in the younger man's heart.

"Surely he is better and stronger," Father Palou said hopefully.

"It is joy that upholds him," a young brother answered.

It was untold joy to have Father Palou with him, Father Serra thought. He could leave all responsibility in his friend's capable hands and make the retreat he wanted with Father Palou's help. Once the retreat was ended, Father Serra acknowledged that he could do no more.

Not that he was an ideal patient. That he never learned to be. He still used his small amount of strength to the uttermost and he was apt to give away even the blanket that was left to cover him. There was a battle royal over the last sacraments.

"Stay here, Father," Father Palou pleaded. "I will deck the place and make it fitting for the coming of our Lord."

"Nonsense, my son. Why should I make His Majesty come here when I can walk to Him?" Father Serra demanded, and he walked to the church clinging to the strong arm of Father Palou.

He vested and knelt at the altar, singing the hymn of St. Thomas Aquinas with all his old fire and love. Voices faltered as the service went on, but his was strong and clear.

Only at the last did he look around with tear-filled eyes at the church he had built and loved.

He came back none the worse for his effort, though he was feeble and weak enough for Father Palou to strive to keep people from exhausting him. His Indians must come, Father Serra insisted, and when he heard the *San Antonio* was in he asked for the officers so that he could hear about his soldiers and sailors from them.

Early in the afternoon he turned to Father Palou. "The pain has lessened," he said. "Help me. I will rest a little."

On the hard little bed he lay smiling contentedly, only asking for his "missionary cross," the crucifix which was always by him, the one which he had lifted high when he landed on the shore of "lost" Monterey, and which he had held aloft as he founded mission after mission.

He was drowsy and fell asleep at once. Father Palou tiptoed out, thinking how peaceful Father Serra seemed.

The hut was very still when Father Palou returned a little later and went over to the bed. How quietly he is resting at last, Father Palou thought, and then he realized that it was a different rest. The long trail had ended. Father Serra had gone home. Father Palou knelt beside him looking at the quiet face and smiling lips while his own tears fell.

The tolling bell brought the galloping *vaqueros* to a standstill and the lads sprang from their horses and knelt to pray as the bell boomed on. The men in the fields heard it and wept for their "old father," as the sound of the guns from the ships joined that of the bells and sailors and soldiers mourned for their friend.

Swift horsemen sped from the mission and the friars came in

haste to do honor to the man who had led them through the years.

Father Palou had little time for the indulgence of his own grief. The sailors besieged him, begging for Father Serra's sandals to use as amulets against the perils of the sea. The Indian neophytes crowded in to plead for a bit of his faded robe and their tears fell upon the scrap of material worn out in their service.

Soldiers and sailors vied with one another for the honor of carrying Father Serra to his last resting place. The Indians had scoured the country for the flowers he loved. These they heaped about him until the casket was hidden by their gifts of love.

The bells tolled and the cannon kept up the sullen booming while those he loved sang the requiem and laid Father Serra to rest by the side of Father Crespi. And surely in the heavenly country the trumpets were sounding for the faithful servant who had come home.

Did Las Palmas still think that his life was wasted? We do not know. Perhaps some of the old professors, who had studied with the brilliant boy from Petra, sighed a little and said he could have gone far. Perhaps some of his Spanish brothers thought regretfully that he could have been the second Bonaventura of their order. They did not realize what he had done.

Father Serra had made the trail to California. He had laid the foundation of a Golden State. He had built not only for his own nation but also for another, a great free country which would stretch from ocean to ocean, whose life lines would cross the continent and bind it into one United States. He had brought fruits, cattle, grain and civilization to a desert land

and a forgotten race. He had made the wilderness blossom as the rose.

Except for his faith and courage again and again the settlements of California would have been lost. Was a country of deserts, lofty mountains, earthquakes and lost harbors worth settling? many had asked. The people are pagan, ignorant, unreliable—are they worth saving after all?

"A thousand times worth while, Father Serra answered, if not in words at least by his work and life. The history of California today might have been very different if the missions had been abandoned.

Father Serra's dream has come true. Today, Los Angeles, Monterey, San Diego, Santa Barbara and the great port of San Francisco are, as he prophesied, the great cities of the Far West. The wealth of California began with the fruits, the flocks, the herds, the ranches and the crops which were started by the sons of St. Francis.

Father Serra was ahead of his time. His ideal was always freedom built on the love of God and man. He had no race prejudice and he fought that evil valiantly when governors and captains would have enslaved the Indians or complained because they were treated the same as the white settlers. There was to be no difference between Indians and colonists, Father Serra maintained, and he saw to it that in the missions there was none.

His greatest achievement is not always so clearly recognized. With his handful of friars he converted the pagans. Thousands of souls were won for God before he died and the work went on long afterward, hampered as the missions were by the Spanish governors.

Junípero Serra is not forgotten. There is a simple grave to be seen at Carmel. It is marked by twisted cypress limbs in the form of a cross and there Father Serra rests before the altar of San Carlos. His statues greet the traveler at Monterey, at San Francisco and beneath the great cross of Malibu.

His missions are still the pride of California, some in ruins, some restored. The bells still ring at San Gabriel and at Carmel-by-the-Sea, pealing out the message of love and faith and courage, the message of the lame friar who blazed the way for generations to come: "No service is too great, no service is too small for the love of God and man."

BIBLIOGRAPHY

BERGER, J. A. *Franciscan Missions in California.*
New York: Doubleday, Doran. 1948

BOLTON, H. *The Spanish Borderlands.*
(Chronicles of America Series.)
Connecticut. Yale University Press. 1921

CLELAND, R. *Pageant of California.*
New York. Knopf. 1946

CULLEN, T. F. *Spirit of Serra.*
New York. Spiritual Book Associates. 1935

DAWSON, G. S. *California, the Story of our Southeast Corner.*
California.

ELLERBE, Rose. *Tales of California Yesterdays*
California. Los Angeles; Warren and Potter. 1916

ENGELHARDT, C. E. *Mission San Carlos Borromeo.*
California. Franciscan Fathers, Mission Santa Barbara. N.D.

FORBES, A. S. C. *California Missions and Landmarks.*
California. Privately printed, Los Angeles. 1903

HERR, Charlotte. *The Mariposa Legend.*
California. Pasadena Post Printing and Binding Co. 1921

O'FARRELL, M. J. *Junipero Serra, Priest and Pioneer.*
New Jersey. St. Antony Guild Press. 1948

PALOU, F. *Founding of the First Californian Mission under the spiritual guidance of Junipero Serra.*
California. Watson. 1934

PALOU, F. *Junipero Serra, Pioneer of California.*
California. Cogan. 1934

REPPLIER, A. *Junipero Serra, Pioneer of California.*
New York. Doubleday, Doran. 1933

SULLIVAN AND LOGIE. *Story of the Spanish Missions of the Southwest.*
New York. (Private Publication.) 1928

SERRA, J. *Diary: an Account of his Journey from Loretto to San Diego. 1789*
Rhode Island. Franciscan Missionaries of Mary. 1935

General works consulted.

THE CATHOLIC ENCYCLOPAEDIA. *Serra, Junipero.*
New York. The Encyclopaedia Press. 1913

THE ENCYCLOPAEDIA BRITANNICA. *California: Majorca and Serra, Junipero.*
New York. 1929. Fourteenth Edition.

For the many pamphlets, magazine articles and other data, sent to me by friends, I give my grateful thanks.

For the basis of the life of Father Serra, in doubtful cases or in contradictions, I have followed Father Palou from whose book I gathered many details.

For the journey to California I depended on Father Serra's own diary which ended with the arrival at San Diego.

The early life of Father Serra had to be gathered from many sources. These included accounts of life on the island of Majorca in books of Spanish history and travel.

INDEX

158

About the Author

IVY BOLTON comes from a long line of writers and poets. Her father was a famous historian and authority on Indian life, and her brother is a well known playwright. Born in England, she came to the United States as a school girl and graduated from Saint Mary's School in Peekskill, New York. At the University of Chicago she took special courses in English. By profession she is a librarian, having graduated from the New York Public Library, but much of her life has been spent in teaching. For eleven years she was Mistress of Studies at Saint Mary's School for Mountain Girls in Sewanee, Tennessee, and until her death in 1960 she taught English and history at her alma mater, and also served as librarian there. Ivy Bolton has written for young people's magazines; has contributed plays for amateur production and is the author of several historical adventure stories for boys and girls.